Published by Spellbound Publishers
Austin, TX
www.spellboundpublishers.com

Copyright © 2017 by Renee Casteel Cook
All rights reserved

Cover design by Tom Kirsch Designs
Layout design by Letitia Smith
Edited by Marcy Stellfox

First published 2017

Manufactured in the United States

ISBN 9780997734942

Library of Congress Control Number: 2017950582

Notice: The information in this book is true and complete to the best of our knowledge. It is offered without guarantee on the part of the author or Spellbound Publishers. The author and Spellbound Publishers disclaim all liability in connection with the use of this book.

All rights reserved. No part of this book may be reproduced or transmitted in any form whatsoever without prior written permission from the publisher except in the case of brief quotations embodied in critical articles and reviews.

A bird doesn't doubt the wind.

Along with the rest of the *Trailer Food Diaries* Series, this book is dedicated to anyone who has ever taken a leap of faith.

CONTENTS

ACKNOWLEDGEMENTS	7
INTRODUCTION	11
BEHIND THE SCENES: FOOD TRUCK COOKBOOKS	15

BREAKFASTS — 19

- Bees Knees Honey Granola *Kinetic* — 20
- The Belmont *The Egg Carton* — 24
- Chorizo Potato Hash *Sunnyside Tacos* — 27
- Popeye Hash *The Egg Carton* — 30

HANDHELDS — 33

- The Al Fresco *Easy Slider* — 34
- Black Bean Quinoa Burger *Fraiche Mobile Kitchen* — 38
- Cali Dreamin' Burger *Street Thyme* — 42
- Cajun Cowboy Hotdog *Bernie's Burger Bus* — 44
- Cajun Flame Burger *Street Thyme* — 48
- Croque Madame *Burro Cheese Kitchen* — 50
- The Festa Italiana *Ole Latte Food Cart* — 54
- Green Shrimp Ceviche Tostada *Rosarito* — 58
- The It's All Gouda *Easy Slider* — 61
- Old World Kielbasa Sandwich with Bourbon Glaze Mustard, Apple Horseradish Slaw and Sophie's Pierogi Garnish *Sophie's Gourmet Pierogi* — 63
- PB & J Banh Mi Sandwich *Ole Latte Food Cart* — 67
- Trafficking Turkey *Paddy Wagon* — 68
- Treasure Island Sushi Roll *Wasabi Sushi* — 71
- The Seared Ahi Tuna *Easy Slider* — 74
- Sherriff's Roll *Paddy Wagon* — 76

COLUMBUS FOOD TRUCK CULTURE: KEVIN BRENNAN AND MIKE GALLICCHIO — 79

MAIN COURSES — 85

- Beef Bacon Cheddar Stuffed Meatballs *Mangiamo Handmade Street Food* — 86
- Brie Stuffed Pierogi with Fried Chicken, Apple Butter and Rosemary, Honey and Pepitas Compound Butter *Sophie's Gourmet Pierogi* — 88
- Cardamom Chai Chicken *DesiPDX* — 92
- Cider Braised Loin Chops *Ray Ray's Hog Pit* — 97
- Chorizo *SunnySide Tacos* — 100
- Crispy Umami Chicken Wings *The Peached Tortilla* — 103
- Green Chile Clam Chowder *Dock & Roll* — 106
- Grilled Hibachi Chicken *Hapa Ramen PDX* — 110
- Guinness Braised Pulled Pork *Mangiamo Handmade Street Food* — 112
- Hawaiian Style Ahi Limu Poke *Hapa Ramen PDX* — 113
- Jumbolaya *Sweet T's Southern Style Food Truck* — 114
- Lamb Bacon *Challah!* — 118
- Lechon Asado *The Guava Tree Truck* — 121
- Melbourne Power Grains Bowl *Kinetic* — 124
- Shrimp & Grits *Sweet T's Southern Style Food Truck* — 126
- Sweet/Sour/Spicy Chicken Wings *Burger Stevens* — 128
- Valentina Ceviche *Rosarito* — 131

SIDES — 133

- Bacon Wrapped Meatballs (a.k.a. Moink Balls) *SLAB BBQ* — 135
- Bacon Wrapped Stuffed Jalapeños (a.k.a. ABTs) *SLAB BBQ* — 137

BBQ Broccoli *Burger Stevens*	138
Black Bean Hummus *Explorer's Club*	140
Boerewors Bites *Fetty's Street Food*	143
Corn Fritters *Burger Stevens*	146
Crab Croquettes *Dock & Roll*	148
Cuban Style Black Beans *The Guava Tree Truck*	151
Elote Salad *Por'Ketta Food Truck*	152
Fried Green Tomatoes *Sweet T's Southern Style Food Truck*	155
Grilled Asparagus with Strawberry Kalonji Dressing & Cumin Fried Hazelnuts *DesiPDX*	157
Hominy Fries *Sweet T's Southern Style Food Truck*	159
Indian Style Radish Quick Pickles *DesiPDX*	161
Kimchi Fries *Chi'Lantro*	162
Latkes *Challah!*	165
Mango Salsa *Tortilla Street Food*	166
Marinated Beets with Black Walnuts *Viking Soul Food*	169
Potato Salad *Challah!*	172
Roasted Red Pepper and Asparagus *Kinetic*	173
Sweet Corn Soufflé *Fetty's Street Food*	174
Troll Snack! *Viking Soul Food*	175

TEXAS FOOD TRUCK CULTURE: CASE ERICKSON AND TIFFANY HARELIK   179

SAUCES   183

Cajun Aioli *Sweet T's Southern Style Food Truck*	184
Creamy Cilantro Sauce *Tortilla Street Food*	185
Pear 'n the Rose City Syrup *Ole Latte Food Cart*	186
Popeye Sauce *The Egg Carton*	187
Raspberry Habanero Jam *The Egg Carton*	188
Remoulade a la New Orleans Dipping Sauce *Dock & Roll*	189
Tomato Jam *Bernie's Burger Bus*	190

DESSERTS   193

Avocado Key Lime Cheesecake *OMG! Cheesecakery*	194
Blueberry Lavender Sauce *OMG! Cheesecakery*	196
Happy Havalina Donut *Gourdough's*	199
Ms. Kahuhu's Pineapple Cilantro Pops *J Pops*	203

PORTLAND FOOD CART CULTURE: KEN WILSON AND STEVEN SHOMLER   207

LIST OF CONTRIBUTING TRUCKS AND CARTS   214

INDEX   215

ABOUT THE AUTHORS   221

ACKNOWLEDGEMENTS
Renee Casteel Cook

A leap of faith made this book and my previous title, *The Columbus Food Truck Cookbook*, possible. So for me, the fact that Tiffany Harelik has used that quote as an acknowledgment across all of her books is more than a coincidence, it's a summation of our serendipitous relationship. A relationship that has grown from a blind email cold call to a two-year co-authorship under her legacy publisher to this title, which she gave me the opportunity to take lead authorship of under her new publishing company, a milestone for both of us.

By incorporating Columbus back into the Trailer Food Diaries family, we strive to overcome the potential for the title to be misconstrued, with the assumption that the mobile food scene has grown to a point where while nomenclature may vary regionally, the industry is united from the Southwest to the Midwest to the Northwest, whether carts, trailers, or trucks. Writing this "Best of" brought me further to the realization that more similarities than differences exist between the communities that foster the entrepreneurial spirit essential to success in a subset of the food industry, which requires not only culinary chops and business acumen but often mechanical savvy. Though each city has its restrictions, from seasonality to regulatory, which affect the way diners become familiar with the when/where/how of mobile dining, these communities have figured out what works best locally, and consumers have discovered that the benefits outweigh any drawbacks mobility may cause.

My gratitude extends to the consumers for supporting what Tiff so perfectly coined as the pursuit of "serving up the American Dream one plate at a time," the cooks and chefs who pursue the dream of sharing their cuisine with those hungry for it (both figuratively and literally), and the communities featured thus far in Trailer Food Diaries for engaging in the mobile food revolution. I use the word "revolution" with my tongue pressed firmly in my cheek as it seems everything comes full circle. Street food has had a long history on most other continents but initially saw resistance in America due to mostly unfounded cleanliness concerns. As the industry has grown from coast to coast in the last few decades, I'm also grateful this issue has dissipated, and we've seen "fast food" turned on its head, bringing along with it incredible diversity, history, and passion from those making it.

This cookbook wouldn't be possible without the support and connections of both Tiffany Harelik and Steven Shomler in their respective home states of Texas and Oregon. Not only did they both embrace and encourage my pursuits from day one, but they also inspired me with their incredible storytelling. They justified my "writing diet" well-balanced through their suggestions of veggie sushi, energy balls, Marcona almonds, kombucha, chocolate milk, crunchy Cheetos, and whiskey and caramel corn without particular concern for proportions or combinations. I added granola due to its health halo and my personal addiction, Italian blood orange tea from my favorite new writing spot (the beautiful Flowers & Bread café), and a bubbly beverage—water or wine—depending on the time of day, I suppose. Association with these two established authors has given me confidence, aspiration, and of course, a strong stomach.

You may also notice that my home market of Columbus, Ohio, is a little more heavily represented in this book, which was somewhat intentional, not because I'm based here but because the scene has continued to grow exponentially from the writing of *The Columbus Food Truck Cookbook*. The other markets are represented by their original role in the series. You'll see a few more trucks from Austin than Portland, and then Dallas and Houston in this book. By no means are we claiming these are the "best" trucks in these markets but rather they represent the "Best of" spirit of the TFD series. In that vein, we've included new trucks that represent the culture of each scene but perhaps came onto it after the original books were written.

On a personal note, I've become part of a new community (now multiple communities), where I've made friends and now have the honor of telling their stories. I'd be remiss to not express gratitude to those in my closest personal circle. This book came together in less than half the time of the first. I appreciate the time given to me by my mother, mother-in-law, and husband in caring for the baby who was still "baking" when we wrote the first book but is now a spirited 18-month-old going on about 18 years. And to that stubborn, determined and already fiercely independent little girl whose first favorite food was a portabella mushroom, I hope you always stay curious in all pursuits but especially the culinary and find exploring cultures and communities through their food as wildly exciting as I do.

I wish the same for anyone who picks up this book—from the readers to the cooks to those that frequent the trucks. Use this as your personal food tour, and don't forget to ask the chefs to sign your copy! The goal is that there's something for each of you in these pages, and I'd love to hear your experiences. Contact me via social media (@RCasteelCook) or at www.reneecasteelcook.com.

INTRODUCTION

Steven Shomler, Portland Food Cart Stories

My name is Steven Shomler, and I love the Portland Food Cart community. I have been writing about it and cheering on food cart owners and consulting with them since early 2012.

I am so excited for you to read this wonderful book that Renee Casteel Cook has put together. This cookbook is the latest volume in an amazing set of culinary books — the Trailer Food Diaries Cookbook series. You are going to love both the profiles and the recipes contained herein.

Since the title of this book is *The Best of Trailer Food Diaries Cookbook,* I wanted to give a little background on the Trailer Food Diaries Cookbook series founder, Tiffany Harelik.

Once in a while, if you are very lucky, someone comes into your life and changes it for the better. Tiffany Harelik has done that for many people. Myself included. A story, please…

In the summer of 2011, I stood in a dirt driveway in Portland, Oregon, and I decided to become an author, writer, and speaker. I was going to leave banking behind and begin a new career.

For more than 20 years, I had wanted to be able to go into a bookstore and buy a book that I wrote. Somehow, someway, I was going make that happen. I also love public speaking, and I was determined to become a professional speaker. The first step I took in this new direction was to become a food writer and Jan 1, 2012, I began writing about food carts. I figured if Anthony Bourdain could be paid to eat and drink, so could I.

Tiffany Harelik was one of the miracles that happened to me along the way. It was November 2012 that Tiffany entered my life.

By then, I had been writing and battling for my dreams for a little over a year. Friends had mocked me, and some had even told me that I would never become an author. That November, Tiffany emailed me and asked me if I wanted to write an "ask a local" chapter for her latest book *Trailer Food Diaries Cookbook: Portland Edition, Volume 1*.

I was out of my mind with joy. Words I wrote were going to be published in a book!

This is the incredible feeling that Tiffany has given to many, many people.

"I would like to feature your Austin Food Trailer in my next book."
"I would like to feature your Houston Food Truck in my next book."
"I would like to feature your Portland Food Cart in my next book."

Scores of people have received an email like that from Tiffany, and because of her, their lives were changed for better.

Her irrepressible passion and inspiring tenacity are the reason you get to enjoy the book that you are holding right now.

In March of 2013, Tiffany spent a week in Portland working on *Trailer Food Diaries Cookbook: Portland Edition, Volume 2*. I got to spend lots of time with her that week taking her to meet many of my friends in the Portland food cart community.

I learned first-hand spending that week with her that she was the real deal. Tiffany loves the hardworking people who bring us the amazing food trailer, food truck, and food cart profiles and recipes you will find in this book.

When my first book came out in April of 2014, *Portland Food Cart Stories*, fittingly, it was Tiffany whose words were found on the foreword on pages 11 and 12. To this day, I am still honored that Tiffany wrote the foreword to my first book.

By the way on April 17, 2014, I went into a bookstore and for the first time in my life, I bought I book that I had written. And yes, I cried like a baby. If you want to more know about that day go to www.TheDayIBecameAnAuthor.com #DreamsDoComeTrue

Tiffany and I even did a book signing together at the world's largest independently owned bookstore, Powell's Books. Beyond that, we remained friends and colleagues. I received a call from her introducing me to the latest author she had taken under her wing, Renee Casteel Cook. Renee and Tiffany were working on *The Columbus Food Truck Cookbook* at the time, and it was during that call that we started talking about a potential collaboration. This book is the result of that call. We put the line out for food trucks, carts, and trailers all over our home markets to contribute, and I'm really proud of what came together under Renee's authorship and Tiffany's guidance.

I invite you to open your heart and enjoy *The Best of Trailer Food Diaries Cookbook*. Years of love and hard work have been stirred in.

Cheers,
Steven Shomler

Speaker, Culinary Storyteller, Consultant

www.TheSpeakerYouWant.com
www.SparkToBonfire.com
www.PortandBeerPodcast.com
www.PortlandCulinaryPodcast.com
www.PortandFoodCartAdventures.com
www.GreatFoodGreatStories.com
www.PortandBeerFestivals.com
www.PortlandBLTWeek.com
www.StevenShomler.com

BEHIND THE SCENES: FOOD TRUCK COOKBOOKS

Tiffany Harelik, Trailer Food Diaries

My first foray into "cookbooking" began in 2007 when I began amassing a collection of heirloom recipes from my family that I wanted to pass down. The project mushroomed into a large collection of stories and ingredients that I warehoused on my laptop for years before creating a word document that served as our keepsake family cookbook. I didn't care about publishing it; the idea was to preserve some family history, pictures and recipes to share with future generations. In the course of editing though, I realized I had a decent formula for writing collaborative cookbooks, and I had a passion for the work, too.

The cookbook hobby grew on me and in 2009, I began Trailer Food Diaries as a blog. After a few months of blogging, I met Chef Shay Spence who introduced me to his father Roy Spence, founding partner at the illustrious GSD&M advertising agency. Roy soon became an integral figure in shaping the Trailer Food Diaries. "Working his way down the corporate ladder" as he will tell you, Roy opened the Royito's hot sauce trailer fashioning his mission after three critical lessons learned from his father:

> 1. Be kind to everyone for you never know what someone is going through.
> 2. Keep it simple.
> 3. Don't do mild.

With these principles guiding his inspiring hot sauce trailer, Roy continues to spread the word about the importance of small businesses. "Our country was founded on mom and pop businesses," he says as he explains why food trailers offer such a great outlet for entrepreneurs of any age to pursue their passions.

A few months later, I pitched a food truck festival concept to C3 Presents. Together, we created the Gypsy Picnic Trailer Food Festival in 2010. With close to thirty food trailers and nearly twenty thousand attendees, we learned just how much Austin loves their food trucks. We did it a second year in 2011 with over thirty thousand attendees, where the first *Trailer Food Diaries Cookbook: Austin Edition, Volume 1* was launched.

Beyond the Gypsy Picnic, I began co-producing Trailer Food Tuesdays, a food truck and live music event held at the Long Center in Austin, Texas, with the city skyline as the backdrop.

At the time of the writing of this volume, I have been all over the world researching outdoor cuisine from food trucks to cowboy ranch cooking, exotic travel, metaphysical lore, and beyond. The notion of street food is worldwide and has its roots in almost every culture. I have eaten street food in Peru, Honduras, Mexico, the British Virgin Islands, Puerto Rico, France, and most of the states in the US. From my experience interviewing people for my cookbooks, I can tell you three key things these folks have in common:

    1. They are entrepreneurs. They do not want to work for anyone else and will work an eighty-hour week for themselves and their family to avoid working a forty-hour week for someone else.

    2. They have at least one good recipe that someone has complimented them on or that they have loved cooking since childhood. It's a recipe they are proud to share with you, and their favorite part of the day is when you take that first bite and your eyes light up. They are cooking to see you smile, not for a grandiose payday.

    3. They are community-oriented people. For the most part, the food truck owners report that one of the things they love most about owning and operating their cart is the opportunity to meet so many

different people during the day. They are as intrigued by your story and what brought you to their food as you are by their menu.

Although we have several editions out in various cities, there are no duplicated recipes in the cookbooks; each cookbook has completely different recipes in it. To date, we have volumes in Austin, Portland, Dallas-Fort Worth, Houston, and now Columbus.

When Renee first contacted me about adding Columbus to the series, she told me she had bought a copy of the *Trailer Food Diaries* and first reached out with a "cold" email in 2014, which resulted in a penpal-like friendship. With her background in advertising and interest in getting started in food writing and my experience with authoring cookbooks, we decided to join forces and learn more about the growing food truck culture in Columbus, Ohio, where she had recently relocated. With the mission of learning her new hometown via food, Renee explored neighborhoods like Clintonville, German Village, the Short North, the campus of Ohio State University, and everything in between.

After adding Columbus to the *Trailer Food Diaries* family, we decided it was time to put together a "Best of the Best" of our favorite food trucks from over the years in our home markets: Texas, Oregon, and Ohio. Included in this book are picks from seasoned food truckers with years under their belts and food truckers that are new to the industry and caught our eyes as noteworthy. We are excited to see where the series will lead us next. I am continually inspired by the pursuit of passion in the food and beverage industry. The recipes in this title are every bit as interesting as the stories behind the food truck chefs. We hope you are inspired, too.

BREAKFASTS

BEES KNEES HONEY GRANOLA KINETIC

THE BELMONT THE EGG CARTON

CHORIZO POTATO HASH SUNNYSIDE TACOS

POPEYE HASH THE EGG CARTON

BEES KNEES HONEY GRANOLA
Courtesy of Andy O'Brien, Kinetic

Makes around 10 cups, crumbled, or enough for about 8 generous bars

INGREDIENTS:
2 1/2 cups rolled oats
3/4 cup whole almonds, roughly chopped
1/4 cup butter, unsalted
1/3 cup honey
1/4 cup packed light brown sugar
1/2 teaspoon vanilla extract
1/4 teaspoon kosher salt
1/2 cup dried cranberries
Small handful of mini chocolate chips

This is a great beginner's recipe for making homemade granola. You can change the recipe to achieve different results by adding peanut butter chips or dried raisins instead of cranberries, etc. You'll definitely be turning heads with this crowd pleaser.

FIRST, line a square baking pan with aluminum foil. Spray the lined pan with non-stick cooking spray. Begin by adding rolled oats and almonds to tray, toast them in the oven at 350º F for 3 to 5 minutes. Stir granola mix and continue baking for 3 to 5 more minutes.

While the oats are toasting, grab a saucepan and begin melting the butter over medium-low heat. Combine the honey, brown sugar, vanilla, and salt. Stir until the mixture is smooth and dissolved. Note: If making granola bars, don't skimp on honey; it helps bind and hold your mix into bars.

When ready, combine the oat and butter mix into a large bowl. Stir the ingredients and then place the mix onto the lined baking sheet. If you are making the granola into bars, place the mix on the baking sheet and press firmly until mix is compact. Chill granola for 1 to 2 hours in the refrigerator then cut into individual bars. Once finished, store the granola at room temperature in a sealed container.

KINETIC *Andy O'Brien*

Staying true to their brand values and passion for making healthy, nutritious foods more accessible at an affordable price, the Kinetic team led by owner Andy O'Brien has evolved the brand and offering while establishing a loyal fan base over the past three years.

Inspired by a family of entrepreneurs and parents who were college athletes, O'Brien has built a team that shares a passion for being the best they can be every day. He and his team extend that philosophy to their customers while embracing the "Kinetic Lifestyle" (one focused on bettering oneself through not only fulfilling food, but also exercise, mental health and motivation, and other healthy habits). A few times a year, the full team is involved in menu ideation and creativity sessions using ingredients from the familiar to the trendy and playing around to conceptualize new items.

The menu format is a build-your-own concept. The West Coast, an original signature dish, remains a crowd pleaser featuring fire-roasted corn, black beans, Monterey jack cheese, a cilantro lime vinaigrette, and avocado on a bed of gluten free power grains and leafy greens topped with tender marinated grilled chicken breast.

O'Brien's personal favorite, the Kineticookie, is the truck's sweet offering. The cookie was developed to provide clean, portable energy while in training for the Pelontonia cycling fundraiser benefitting cancer research at Ohio State University's James Cancer Hospital. "When my friends found out that I created a healthy cookie that also tastes good, they all wanted some too, and eventually the cookie became a staple on our truck!" recalls O'Brien.

Another key member of the team is the truck itself that even has a friendly moniker. Paying homage to one of the truck's first customers, they named the truck Kendra and keep her order ticket (for a banana smoothie) posted in the truck as a reminder of how far they've come.

Next up for the Kinetic crew? They've decided to launch a healthy meal prep service based on customer demand. The service will feature favorite menu items from the truck alongside some unique meal preparations and allow followers an easy way to enjoy great Kinetic meals even when they're away from the truck.

THE BELMONT
Courtesy of Sarah and Tim Arkwright, The Egg Carton

This popular sandwich uses our raspberry habanero jam. The measurements for the sandwiches are approximate, so in my family, I load up extra goat cheese and jam while my Midwest meat-loving husband gets extra meat. You could substitute regular raspberry jam if you can't eat spicy foods.

Serves 4

INGREDIENTS:
4 biscuits (we use our own cart made buttermilk biscuits)
12 slices of Canadian bacon, ham, or prosciutto
Arugula
4 ounces goat cheese, crumbled
One jar of Raspberry Habanero Jam (page 188)
4 eggs, fried over medium

ON A HOT GRIDDLE, split open the biscuits and lightly toast the insides.

Cook the Canadian bacon, ham, or prosciutto until browned and lightly crisp.

Assemble the sandwiches with approximately 1/2 to 1-ounce goat cheese, up to 3 slices of meat, arugula, a spread of jam, and an over medium fried egg.

THE EGG CARTON *Sarah & Tim Arkwright*

After five years of working together day in and day out, Sarah Arkwright jokes that she and husband Tim should count their wedding anniversaries as double. As they expand operations of The Egg Carton to serve seven days a week, that may even increase. So far, they've enjoyed the transition from retail sales for her and the legal profession for him to serving their South East Portland neighborhood and the success it has brought them as entrepreneurs.

Their story starts somewhat classically. Sarah had recently experienced a layoff. One morning, they found themselves standing in line for brunch and realized the lack of breakfast carts in their neighborhood. Sarah's a self-trained cook. During a year the couple was primarily homebound due to an illness Tim successfully fought, Sarah relied on cookbooks, YouTube, and many hours spent in the kitchen to hone her skills. Fully recovered now, Tim runs operations including finances, inventory, and purchasing while his wife commands the front of the house, cooking and serving. But that doesn't mean he's not involved in menu creation. His love for biscuits and gravy and the epic snowstorm of 2014 (which had them snowed in for three days) led to the invention of their current sell-out special. Served on the weekends only, the dish leverages the spicy sausage they had been serving on breakfast sandwiches in a new way. In an ironic twist, Sarah's not a lover of the classic dish and didn't want to commit to making it a permanent menu item based on the labor required to make the seven quarts of gravy required for the dish.

She also doesn't eat biscuits except in her own kitchen, but after perfecting her recipe, she acquiesced to her husband's begging and now sells around one hundred biscuits per day.

Sarah's homemade jams are another signature item and are also available by the jar from the truck. Featuring flavors like raspberry habanero, blueberry vanilla basil, and marionberry, a flavor unique to Oregon.

Over the years, the Arkwright's have seen both growth and attrition in the Portland food truck scene describing it as "really ramshackle with carts opening and closing often." As the city experiences an incredible growth spurt, the price of land is increasing and cart paths are getting demolished as developers see value in building in new areas. To stand the test of time in current market conditions, Sarah notes that many trucks are now choosing to concentrate on one thing that they do really well, such as a neighboring cart dedicated to Russian dumplings.

The Egg Carton's focus on high quality, handmade breakfast sandwiches has gained them recognition locally. Sarah's 2015 appearance on the Food Network's Chopped program, which was also shown on Southwest flights into Portland for about a year after, gained the business further exposure and brought out-of-towners in to check things out. While the Arkwright's are conservative about their business plan, their loyal following consistently asks when they'll open a brick and mortar, which they're open to doing. But for now, they're happy to grow their team by expanding cart operations and continue to increase visibility as one of Portland's top mobile food offerings.

CHORIZO POTATO HASH
Courtesy of Joshua Di Bari, Sunnyside Tacos

Use your favorite potato—Russet, red, or sweet or a combination of all three—to build a hash as beautiful as it is flavorful.

Serves 4

INGREDIENTS:
2 pounds potatoes
1 tablespoon olive oil
1 tablespoon bacon or pork fat (optional)
Salt and pepper
12 ounces of chorizo
1 medium onion, diced
2 jalapeño or 1 poblano pepper, seeded and diced (optional)
4 eggs
1 bunch parsley, to garnish
1 ounce herbs (chives recommended), to garnish
4 ounces queso fresco, for garnish

BEGIN hash by dicing potatoes and blanching them in water until they are halfway cooked, approximately 7-10 minutes or until a fork inserts easily. Let them cool and air dry. In the meantime, heat the olive oil and pork fat in a heavy frying pan. Place the potatoes in the frying pan and season with salt and pepper. As they start to brown and become crispy, place them on one side of the pan and turn the heat to medium.

On the other side of the pan, add the ground chorizo and cook until finished, then add the onions and peppers. Mix the potatoes and chorizo together and cook for another 1 to 2 minutes to allow the potatoes to absorb the flavor from the chorizo. In a separate pan, poach an egg or cook it in whatever manner suits you.

Put the potato, chorizo, onion, and pepper mixture on a separate plate. Garnish with parsley, fresh herbs, and queso fresco, then place the egg on top of the hash.

* * *

SUNNYSIDE TACOS *Joshua Di Bari*

A staff meal at a Michelin-rated Chicago restaurant was where Joshua Di Bari first found inspiration for what would become Sunnyside Tacos. As his affinity for Mexican food— specifically authentic street tacos—developed so did his intrigue with charcuterie, specifically pork. Learning to use every part of the animal, he discovered the versatility of sausage and how it can be prepared and used in so many different cuisines.

Taking note of the evolution of the restaurant industry back in his hometown of Columbus, Di Bari decided to move back and partner with Richard Rieth, a friend since elementary school, to unite their skill sets and launch Sunnyside Tacos in 2015. Di Bari specifically appreciates Columbus because the "culinary and consumer scene is very much focused on local produce and meat in large part due to the fact that there are great farms within an easy drive."

His personal favorites, the torta and the Mexican beans, use both meat and local produce. The torta features a custom torta roll made specifically for Sunnyside by Matt Swint of Matija Breads, bean purée, smoked ham, braised crispy pork belly, queso Chihuahua, onions, cilantro, lettuce, mayo, and salsa verde. The Mexican beans, which Di Bari says are the Mexican version of French cassoulet, have every part of the pig—ham, carnitas, pork belly, skin, chorizo—plus loads of vegetables and herbs, cooked in a flavorful brazing liquid and served with chips. Di Bari hopes these signature dishes showcase the flavor, texture, and skill that is the basis of Sunnyside Tacos.

A current customer favorite, the smoked chicken taco, contains cured chicken thighs that are smoked over a blend of fruitwood chips with poblano peppers, onions, garlic, tomatoes, and jalapeños.

"Columbus is a big city that is experiencing tremendous growth but still has a Midwest feel," Di Bari says happy to be back home. "Everyone is nice, helpful. And the four seasons and long grow season give us a diverse and abundant crop which is always key to supporting local farmers. Along with the large art, music, and craft beer following, there are always opportunities for food trucks and carts to feed people."

POPEYE HASH

Courtesy of Sarah and Tim Arkwright, The Egg Carton

This is a great hearty breakfast and is gluten and dairy free. I adapted it from a popular recipe for just the sweet potatoes cooked with rosemary (which can also be found in "Trailer Food Diaries: Portland Volume 2")—a great side dish!

Serves 2

INGREDIENTS:

2 cups white sweet potatoes, parboiled and diced into 1/2-inch cubes,
Canola oil
1/2 cup bacon, roughly chopped
Salt and pepper
1 tablespoon fresh rosemary
1/2 cup tomatoes, diced
1/2 cup fresh baby spinach
Popeye sauce (page 187)
4 eggs cooked over easy (or any style)
1 avocado, sliced (optional)

TO PARBOIL the potatoes, put the potatoes in a large pan and cover with cold water.

Bring the water to a boil over high heat. As soon as the water starts to boil, turn the heat off but keep the pan on the burner. Let the pan of potatoes stand on the burner for about 5 minutes, depending on the size of the potatoes. Larger potatoes may need more standing time. Drain all of the water from the pan. Allow potatoes to cool enough to handle then dice into 1/2-inch cubes. Store the potatoes in a bowl in the refrigerator until ready to use.

To make the hash, coat the bottom of a large pan with canola oil and heat to medium high. Place the bacon in the pan and cook until just starting to brown, then add the prepared sweet potatoes. Season the mixture generously with salt and pepper and add the rosemary.

Add the tomatoes and spinach and toss gently until the spinach is barely wilted.

Place the hash on two plates and top with a generous drizzle of Popeye sauce, 2 eggs, and avocado slices.

HANDHELDS

THE AL FRESCO EASY SLIDER

BLACK BEAN QUINOA BURGER FRAICHE MOBILE KITCHEN

CALI DREAMIN' BURGER STREET THYME

CAJUN COWBOY HOTDOG BERNIE'S BURGER BUS

CAJUN FLAME BURGER STREET THYME

CROQUE MADAME BURRO CHEESE KITCHEN

THE FESTA ITALIANA OLE LATTE

GREEN SHRIMP CEVICHE TOSTADA ROSARITO

THE IT'S ALL GOUDA EASY SLIDER

OLD WORLD KIELBASA SANDWICH WITH BOURBON GLAZE MUSTARD, APPLE HORSERADISH SLAW AND SOPHIE'S PIEROGI GARNISH SOPHIE'S GOURMET PIEROGI

PB & J BANH MI SANDWICH OLE LATTE

TRAFFICKING TURKEY PADDY WAGON

TREASURE ISLAND SUSHI ROLL WASABI SUSHI PDX

THE SEARED AHI TUNA EASY SLIDER

SHERRIFF'S ROLL PADDY WAGON

THE AL FRESCO
Courtesy of Caroline Perini, Easy Slider

The American classic goes Italian and bite size.

Serves 1

INGREDIENTS:
Olive oil
1 slice prosciutto
3 ounces Angus beef, formed into a patty
Sea salt
Slider bun
4 cherry tomatoes
2 leaves fresh basil, torn
1 teaspoon aged balsamic vinegar
1 slice burrata cheese, sliced 1/2-inch thick

HEAT a hot griddle top to high. Place 2 tablespoons of olive oil onto the hot griddle top. Place the prosciutto slice onto the griddle. Lightly fry the prosciutto until golden and firm. Set aside.

Add the Angus patty onto the hot griddle. The griddle should be hot enough to cause the patty to sizzle, thus ensuring a crusted sear. Sear one side of the Angus beef patty and let it cook for approximately 3 minutes. Lightly season with sea salt.

Once the patty begins to brown along the edges, use a spatula to flip the beef patty. Using the back and heel of the spatula, press firmly and "smash" the beef patty into the griddle.

Let slider rest and cook for approximately 4 more minutes. Meanwhile, toast slider bun.

To assemble the cherry tomato salad, slice the cherry tomatoes in half,

chop the fresh basil and drizzle with the aged balsamic vinegar. Sprinkle sea salt to taste.

Place the slice of burrata cheese onto cooked Angus beef patty. Place cooked Angus beef patty onto toasted, bottom slider bun. Onto toasted top bun, spoon approximately 1 tablespoon cherry tomato salad.

Cover cherry tomato salad with the piece of crispy prosciutto. Flip dressed top bun onto the Angus beef patty, ensuring all ingredients stay together and intact.

Garnish with a cherry tomato speared with a toothpick through the top bun.

EASY SLIDER *Caroline Perini*

"To me, food trucks are the modern-day chuck wagon," says Caroline Perini, adding, "It bums me out when people call it a 'trend' as they've been around forever and I don't believe they're going anywhere."

Certainly not in her hometown of Dallas, Texas. Recently, Perini opened the first Easy Slider brick-and-mortar restaurant adding to her fleet of three trucks of the same name. She also owns two other food cart concepts, Open Road Shaved Ice and Bar Cart, a mobile bar service. Though continuing to grow her presence, she shies away from calling her business an empire.

"When we first started Easy Slider we were just hustling as hard as we could, picking up every shift, parking in every parking lot, taking every opportunity to be open," says Perini. But her idea of a "boutique" operation grew rapidly. She added a second truck in less than a year and then a third one. "Our goal was always to have a brick-and-mortar restaurant; we just didn't know how long that would take," she recalls.

As the mobile part of her operation grew and catering became nearly 70% of the business, creating a home base became more feasible. She's excited to have a roof over her head, air conditioning, a patio, and a full bar (which Bar Cart is currently servicing). But the philosophy and core menu haven't changed as Perini still focuses on using the same high-quality meats and freshly baked bread.

This includes 100% Angus beef alongside new protein options like turkey sliders, seared Ahi tuna (which she shares here), and vegetarian options including the baby Portobello mushroom (marinated in a house made vinaigrette and topped with pesto, mozzarella and tomato), and the Hippie Hippie Steak, a cauliflower steak seared with lemon feta vinaigrette and tossed with arugula, pepitas, and dried cranberries.

Perini gets creative with a featured slider of the month, creating a following that has customers waiting all year for their favorite to come back. From the Mini Mac complete with sesame seed bun to the Steakhouse Patty Melt, featuring a slider-sized patty melt on a sourdough bun topped with a house made steak sauce, the offerings are sometimes seasonal and other times tied to her personal preferences (like her love for patty melts). In either case, Perini says they're "a fun way to stretch our legs and keep us on our toes."

While Perini likes to experiment and have fun, her focus never wavers from the original intention to create the perfect bite. Even her wackiest combinations have become signatures like the Sweet and Low Down, a special Perini thought would never last based on its unlikely combination of Angus beef with strawberry jam, goat cheese, and bacon. Her personal twist? Adding jalapeños for a little bit of spice, which makes it her all-time, hands down favorite.

BLACK BEAN QUINOA BURGER

Courtesy of Kristen Schafbuch, Fraiche Mobile Kitchen

Makes roughly 6 patties

INGREDIENTS:

1/2 yellow onion, diced
1 red pepper, diced
Grapeseed oil, for cooking
1 tablespoon cumin
1 tablespoon garlic
1/4 jalapeño (or more for more heat), diced
Salt and pepper
1/2 bunch cilantro
1 can black beans, drained and rinsed
1 cup bread crumbs or cracker crumbs
1 cup cooked rainbow quinoa
Hamburger buns and toppings of your choice

On a meatless Monday (or for your vegan friends and family), cook these up, and you will forget ground beef was ever a thing.

SAUTÉ diced onion and red pepper in a pan with grapeseed oil until tender. Add cumin, garlic, jalapeño, salt and pepper. Let the mixture cool then purée in a food processor with cilantro until chunky (do not over blend to paste). Transfer the mixture to a mixing bowl.

Blend the black beans into a paste and add to puréed vegetables. In an electric mixer set on low, combine the bread crumbs and quinoa together with the puréed black beans and vegetables until a firm (not wet) mixture is formed.

Form patties with the black bean mixture with your hands or by using an egg ring. Make each patty about 1/4-inch thick and 3-inches round. Note: the patties cook better if they have been chilled for about 30 minutes before cooking.

Heat skillet, add a douse of grapeseed oil. Once the oil is hot, add the patties and cook them over medium to high heat. Cook until the patties darken, about 4 minutes on each side. The patty will form a nice sear when it's ready to flip.

Serve black bean patties with all the fixings used with their meat counterparts.

FRAICHE MOBILE KITCHEN
Kristen Schafbuch

Classically trained and with a degree in restaurant management, Kristen Schafbuch took her first job as head pastry chef in 2008. It wasn't until she moved to Houston in 2010 that she tapped into her savory side, opening Fraiche Mobile Kitchen in 2012. Then in 2014, she relocated herself and the business to Austin.

"Every food truck city is its own beast," Schafbuch says. Even though she was a seasoned food truck owner in Houston, she essentially started over in Austin, especially regarding networking, marketing, and most importantly, finding the best locations. But the food and truck operations were the easier part, and with a passion for tackling new projects, Schafbuch was up to the challenge saying she "likes change, and Austin is a thriving and changing city."

The city has embraced her culinary style which she deems a "blend of comfort food with a twist." Showcased in dishes like the best-selling carnitas hash, which features "a beautiful bowl of seasonal farmers market vegetables, local pork, farm fresh eggs, and tater tots." Schafbuch says that "people come back for it, again and again." Her personal favorite? The whiskey-infused waffle, which is topped with juicy fried chicken or a side of pork belly. "Even though I am a pastry chef, I love savory food. And the combo of sweet and salty is pretty much what I live for. It will knock your socks off."

It's clear that Schafbuch is passionate both about her food and the industry as a whole. She has fond memories of her experience as part of the Houston food truck scene and has continued her love of the community in Austin. Of course, uprooting her business and moving cities were big challenges, but the freedom to do so is part of what appeals to her most about the mobile food scene.

Beyond that accomplishment, Schafbuch is proud to run her own

business cooking what she wants and "sourcing food locally to let the ingredients shine for themselves." Though trained to work in fine dining, she enjoys cooking from the heart, especially when customers are "genuinely surprised that the food came off a food truck, or if we cater a wedding and they come back to the window and tell me that was the best wedding food they have ever had."

The customer feedback motivates Schafbuch as does the energy she gets driving the truck and the new menus she concepts. She says, "This industry is where I thrive. I really can't imagine doing anything else."

CALI DREAMIN' BURGER
Courtesy of Alex Emrich, Street Thyme

Avocado and jalapeño top a classic combination of BBQ, cheddar cheese, and bacon to add a West Coast twist.

Serves 2
INGREDIENTS:
2 slices thick cut bacon
2/3 pound ground beef
1 teaspoon kosher salt
1 teaspoon black pepper
1 fresh tomato
1 fresh avocado
1 fresh jalapeño
Romaine lettuce
2 challah roll burger buns
BBQ sauce, to taste
4 slices sharp cheddar cheese

PLACE a non-stick pan on the stovetop and heat for a few minutes over medium heat. Place the bacon in the pan and cook to desired doneness. Chef's note: we prefer medium.

Next, put the ground beef in a mixing bowl and add the salt and pepper. Mix to combine. Make 4 even patties, about 1/6-pound each.

Slice the tomato, avocado, jalapeño, and lettuce.

Remove the bacon from the pan and toast the challah buns in the bacon fat. Toast for approximately 40 seconds, and remove the buns to a plate.

Next, add the burger patties to the warm pan and cook about 75% of the way through, then flip the patties and continue cooking them. Immediately add the cheese and let it melt.

Now stack the burgers double and put the bacon on top. Next, add plenty of avocado, a few slices of jalapeño, drizzled BBQ sauce, lettuce, and tomato.

STREET THYME *Alex Emrich*

In a way, Alex Emrich was destined to run a burger-focused food truck. Following his family lineage, with one grandfather a farmer in Eastern Ohio and the other, a butcher in Columbus, it's possible that the latter finished the former's product before they'd ever even met.

Carrying forward that philosophy and trying to support the local economy, Street Thyme sources its meat from longtime local Italian butcher Carfagnas and gets both its bread and produce locally when available. Those ingredients go into offerings like the customer favorite Apple Bacon Brie Burger (recipe found in *The Columbus Food Truck Cookbook*) and Alex's personal favorite, Pork Belly on a Stick, which a chef friend taught him to make. This special features Ohio pork, seared and braised, served with a chili garlic caramel, and topped with cilantro and chives.

This spirit of chefs teaching chefs is common in Columbus, according to Emrich, who says Columbus has a sort of "interconnectedness about it...people here are very helpful toward each other, even in the same industry. We're all kind of rooting for each other. There are a lot of people trying to accomplish big goals here and [are] proud to call it [Columbus] home, including myself."

Emrich gives shout-outs to former co-workers Steve Carmean and Alex Martin from the Blu Olive food truck where he got his start and also friend and on-call mechanic, Glen, without whom he says Street Thyme (a 1978 Chevrolet) would probably cease to exist.

Emrich furthers his family's local legacy by paying homage to childhood favorites like his mom's meatloaf (still hands down his favorite thing ever) and his dad's grilled burgers topped with Grandma McElroy's homemade dill pickle (the best tasting dill pickle he has ever had). Emrich considers the day a success when customers say they've enjoyed their food, or write glowing reviews, or he's notified of an award like his most recent—second place in the 2016 Best Bites Competition.

CAJUN COWBOY HOTDOG
Courtesy of Justin Turner, Bernie's Burger Bus

Serves 2

INGREDIENTS:
2 tablespoons olive oil
1 bell pepper, sliced
1 large onion, sliced
All purpose flour, for dredging
Peanut oil, for frying
Salt and pepper
2 hot dogs or sausages of your choice
2 hot dog buns, buttered on both sides

Redneck Remoulade:
1 cup mayonnaise (recommend Duke's)
1/2 cup hot salsa
3 tablespoons blackened redfish seasoning (like Paul Prudhomme's Blackened Redfish Magic)
2 tablespoons Worcestershire sauce
1 tablespoon fresh dill, finely chopped
1 teaspoon kosher salt
Hot sauce, to taste

This Bernie's favorite was featured in the Houston CityBook for Super Bowl LI.

START by making remoulade. Mix the mayonnaise and the hot salsa. Add the remaining ingredients and mix well. Cover and chill at least 30 minutes or preferably overnight. Set out the remoulade 1 hour before use.

Heat the olive oil in a frying pan on a stove until very hot. Add the bell pepper to the hot oil and sauté until the pepper is caramelized. Set aside and keep warm.

Lightly dredge the onions in the flour and fry in peanut oil heated to 350º F until golden brown or about 3 minutes. Drain the onions on a paper towel and season with salt and a lot of black pepper.
Split hot dogs or sausages down the middle and grill them on medium-high heat, searing well on both sides. At the same time, grill hot dog buns on both sides.

Place grilled sausages or hot dogs in the toasted buns. Top the grilled meat with caramelized peppers, Redneck Remoulade, and fried onions.

BERNIE'S BURGER BUS *Justin Turner*

Seven years ago, Justin Turner set out to open his own business naming it after his grandfather Bernie. With a fully baked business plan that involved an eventual brick-and mortar-location, he entered the mobile food scene to build his brand, generate awareness, and conduct market research learning what worked and what didn't across various Houston neighborhoods. As he opens his third brick-and-mortar spot in 2017, he's staying true to his original concept and core value of made from scratch, high-quality burgers and accompaniments.

Working in the past as both a fine dining and private chef to a Houston-area basketball player, Turner knew he wanted to do something familiar to people, but really, really well. He considered both hot dogs and pizza before the alliteration hit him—Bernie's Burgers. Not wanting to add "truck" to the end of the name of the business, he went looking for buses and upon finding a school bus, the theme for Bernie's Burger Bus came together almost instantly.

Playing on childhood memories, Bernie named his dishes after the usual suspects from his time in school like the Principal and the Cheerleader. French fries fall into the Extracurricular Activities category of the menu, and the bar areas at his brick-and-mortar spots are known as the Teacher's Lounge. A monthly Field Trip features a special burger, fries, and milkshake offering often conceived by members of the 65-person staff. However, Turner develops the final recipe.

Turner goes back time and time again to the second burger he crafted from the truck, The Substitute, his personal favorite. It's a Danish-style blue cheese burger with tipsy onions (deglazed with Jack Daniels) and burgundy mushrooms, plus applewood smoked bacon. He says the "mushrooms are earthy and yet tart, and perfectly combine with the sweet and tanginess of blue cheese and the saltiness of the bacon."

Gaining popularity quickly, Bernie's expanded to a total of three trucks plus an outpost at the Texans football stadium within the first four years of operation. But Turner's focus was still on a permanent location and deciding to go all in upon opening his first spot, Turner has taken the truck off the road for the last few years. Each restaurant still has a bus inside, which houses the kitchen with an identical setup to the original truck. Turner also kept one truck and sees a possibility to bring it back into service mainly for private events and larger festivals.

After opening his third spot, Turner expects to sell roughly nine thousand burgers per week, which requires prep of 2,100 pounds of onions for caramelization, netting approximately 700 pounds when cooked down. To meet this demand, he invested in a commissary kitchen at his first location with large scale equipment crucial when making things like ketchup and mustard in house. "It's a painstakingly hard process to keep up with but awesome because it differentiates us. Truly no one else can have our burger because we grind our own meat and make all of our own condiments," Turner says. He even has a twist of fate connection to the local baker he uses for his buns. He found Slow Dough Bakery when they were both small and starting out. With his strong taste memory, Turner realized the owner was the son of a baker from Deerfield, Illinois, where Turner's grandmother lived and a place he had visited growing up.

Turner says there's more to come, not only serving burgers in Houston but possibly expanding geographically and crafting new concepts with the same core philosophy. "I'm about to break out and do some cool things," he says, "just as soon as Bernie's slows down just a little, maybe."

CAJUN FLAME BURGER
Courtesy of Alex Emrich, Street Thyme

A savory mixture of heat gives the Cajun Flame Burger its edge.

Serves 2

AIOLI:
1/2 cup of olive oil-based mayonnaise
1 tablespoon sriracha hot sauce
1 teaspoon of habanero-based hot sauce
Salt and pepper

INGREDIENTS:
2/3 pound ground beef
1 teaspoon kosher salt
1 teaspoon black pepper
1 tablespoon butter
2 challah roll burger buns
2 slices of tomato, sliced in large rounds
4 slices hot pepper cheese
2 pinches of shredded lettuce
1 fresh jalapeño, thinly sliced

TO MAKE the habanero sriracha aioli, place the mayonnaise in a mixing bowl, add the sriracha sauce and the habanero hot sauce plus a pinch of salt and pepper. Whisk the ingredients together until they are evenly mixed.

Place a non-stick pan on the stovetop and heat for a few minutes over medium.

Place the ground beef in a mixing bowl and add the salt and pepper. Make 4 even-sized patties, about 1/6-pound each.

Put the butter in the pan and buns on top. Once the butter has melted, wait approximately 40 seconds then remove toasted buns and put them on a plate. Place 2 tomato slices in the pan immediately followed by the 4 burger patties, so they're all in the pan together. Wait until the burgers are cooked about 75% of the way through and then flip the patties. Leave the tomatoes untouched. Immediately add one slice of cheese to each patty, wait for the cheese to melt and stack the patties one on top of another to make two stacks. Use your spatula and put the tomato on the burger, charred side up.

Place each burger stack on the toasted bread.

Place 7 thinly sliced jalapeños on each burger and add as much habanero-sriracha aioli as you'd like. Finish the burger by placing a pinch of lettuce on top of the aioli.

CROQUE MADAME
Courtesy of Justin Turner, Burro Cheese Kitchen

Serves 1
INGREDIENTS:
2 slices sourdough bread
3 to 4 slices smoked ham
3 ounces shredded gouda cheese
olive oil
1 egg
unsalted butter, melted

PESTO:
3 ounces fresh basil
3 ounces almonds
3 ounces parmesan
6 cloves garlic
3 teaspoons Worcestershire sauce
1 1/2 teaspoons black pepper

AIOLI:
1/4 cup extra virgin olive oil (EVOO)
3 tablespoons vegetable oil
1 large egg yolk
2 cloves garlic, minced
2 teaspoons fresh lemon juice
1/2 teaspoon Dijon mustard

DULCE DE LECHE:
Makes 40 ounces
1 gallon whole milk
4 1/2 cups sugar
4 ounces Madagascar vanilla

This is an elevated grilled cheese combining the flavors of sourdough, smoked ham, gouda cheese, pesto aioli and dulce de leche, all topped with a fried egg.

TO MAKE the pesto combine basil, almonds, parmesan, garlic, Worcestershire sauce, and black pepper in a food processor. Purée until the mixture is smooth.

Next, make aioli by combining the extra virgin olive oil and vegetable oil in a bowl. Add the combined oils a few drops at a time to the egg yolk, whisking constantly, until all the oil is incorporated and mixture is emulsified. Add the garlic, lemon juice, and mustard and whisk together until everything is incorporated.

To combine the pesto and the aioli, use a large spoon to fold them together until well combined. Chill the mixture after preparation for serving.

To make the dulce de leche, combine the milk, sugar, and vanilla in a heavy saucepan and stir them together. Over low heat, slowly bring the milk mixture up to a boil, reduce the heat, and simmer uncovered while stirring occasionally.

As the mixture begins to caramelize, stir more often to avoid scorching the bottom of the pan. Keep reducing the milk for approximately 2 hours or until it is light tan in color. Once the sauce has finished reducing, discontinue the heat.

Place a chinois (fine strainer) lined with a cone fryer filter over a 4-quart container, and pour the sauce through the filter to strain out any impurities. Chill the mixture after preparation for serving. The left over dulce de leche can be stored in the refrigerator for approximately 10 days.

To assemble the sandwich, heat a panini press preset to 380º F.

On a sheet pan, select two evenly sized slices of fresh sourdough bread and open them up. Take two ounces of the dulce de leche and spread on one slice evenly. Take 2 ounces of pesto aioli and spread on the opposing slice evenly.

Bring a cast iron flat griddle to medium heat on the stovetop and place 3 to 4 slices of smoked ham on it and sear for about 30 to 45 seconds. Then place 1 teaspoon of olive oil on the same griddle and place 1 large egg on the griddle, frying it over easy.

Place the cooked ham on the dulce de leche covered slice, and place fried egg on top of that. On the sourdough slice with the pesto aioli, place 3 ounces of shredded gouda cheese evenly spread over the entire piece.

Take a brûlée torch, and pre-melt the cheese until you see a slight browning on the melted surface.

Close up the sandwich and with a butter brush, evenly brush on melted, unsalted butter on both sides. Then place sandwich on the panini press for about 45 seconds. Flip the sandwich over for even cooking, and grill for another 45 seconds until the sandwich reaches a rich golden brown color with nice caramelization on the edges.

BURRO CHEESE KITCHEN *Justin Burrow*

For Justin Burrow, it all started at Beecher's in Pike Place Market. He was running a high-end European furniture design showroom in Seattle and would sneak away as often as possible to watch the cheese being made and enjoy the market's flagship cheddar cheese sandwich right next to where the curds were stirred. As he experimented with adding spreads from the market to customize his sandwich, the concept came together in his mind. Then a move back to his hometown, Austin, made it a reality.

Building upon the idea of taking a good cheese plate and putting it into a grilled cheese format, Burrow began developing homemade spreads such as the balsamic apricot fig, meant to bring out the flavor of the cheese it's paired with. Crafting a balance between sweet, savory, spicy, and umami components, Burrow rotates the seasonal menu around six sandwiches as well as a build your own option for endless combinations.

The Croque Madame is a personal favorite inspired by trips to Paris uniquely combining pesto aioli and dulce de leche to offset the salty ham and gouda cheese. A customer favorite (so much so that people have gotten mad if it's not on the menu), the Waylon & Willy, combines spicy maple bacon sauce, diced pepperoncini, rosemary caramelized onions, and aged cheddar on sourdough bread baked by local favorite Easy Tiger.

These offerings can be enjoyed from either of the two Burro trucks or at the original location, a stationary shipping container, which Burrow built out himself truly wanting to know every part of the business. He was one of the first in Austin to leverage the container this way and has not only added a second container location but was awarded the 14th spot on the Top Twenty-Five Food Truck Designs list in *Paste* magazine.

And the name? At first glance, it may appear as a simple play on Burrow's surname, but in fact, it's a nod to the most expensive cheese in the world, Pule, a Serbian cheese from donkey's (translated in Spanish to "burro") milk which retails for $750 per pound. While restrictions on importing raw milk have thus far prohibited Burrow from serving the most expensive grilled cheese in the world, he felt the name spoke well to the concept of elevating the humble grilled cheese to something truly artisan.

THE FESTA ITALIANA
Courtesy of Todd Edwards, Ole Latte

This recipe is a tribute to both the fantastic cultural festival that happens in Pioneer Square every year and the classic Italian sandwich but with a balance between meat and vegetables.

Serves 1
1 plain bagel, toasted if desired
1 1/2 ounces ham
1 1/2 ounces pastrami
1 slice provolone cheese
3 to 4 rings red onion
5 to 6 sundried tomatoes with oil
Arugula, a handful or to taste
Oregano
Red chili flakes

HEAT a skillet or griddle over high heat. Sear the ham and pastrami. Place the provolone cheese slice on top to keep the meats hot and melt the provolone.

Add the red onions, sliced thin, and spread them evenly across the face of the sandwich.

Add the sundried tomatoes with a little oil in even distribution onto the sandwich. The tomato oil helps to keeps the sandwich from becoming too dry.

Grab a handful of arugula and crush it into a ball in your hand condensing it. Add the arugula to the sandwich. To finish, cover the sandwich with the desired amount of oregano and red chili flakes.

OLE LATTE *Todd Edwards*

Keeping Portlanders caffeinated since 2012, Todd Edwards now serves the city through three carts and a brick and mortar. Raised in Portland, he returned after stints in California, Georgia, and Alabama, for what he says is "the pure beauty of the state," and takes to the outdoors as a way to "refill his batteries and embrace nature." Locals recharge their batteries with his best-selling offerings like the seasonal signature latte and secret (off-menu) peanut butter banh mi sandwich, which he shares here.

A restaurant and hospitality industry veteran for almost two decades, Edwards worked his way up from host to manager before deciding to take his experiences "both good and bad," and start his own business realizing a long-time dream. His success is based on these best practices along with the tight food cart community, which provides support and shares ideas. Edwards loves that "everyone seems to see the bigger picture and wants to help in any way. When things don't work one way, it is abandoned, and a new way is adopted quickly to keep the energy creative to progress our city."

The culinary progress in Portland owes much credit to the nearly

perfect micro-climate that can grow just about anything and allows for excellent choices in local sourcing. Edwards says Portlanders as a whole "collaborate and support each other because we all have so much passion for growing our little city. Don't be afraid if someone smiles and asks about your day. We truly are interested without ulterior motives."

He's even positive about the challenges of the mobile food scene while he acknowledges that "a food cart restricts logistics which requires you to keep mentally up with stock and demand." He spins this positive saying "the same problem is also rewarding because none of your stock really starts to go bad." Further Edwards adds, "...since they [food carts] are so small, you are restricted in everything from supplies, [to] water, electricity, and waste, but that downside also provides us...with a low carbon footprint."

And it's not just the caffeine buzz talking. Edwards's go-to libation is his Alhemp Latte, a blend of almond and hemp milks that's not too hemp-y or almond-y and has a wonderful texture similar to whole milk.

GREEN SHRIMP CEVICHE TOSTADA
Courtesy of Carlos Acosta, Rosarito

This street food delicacy combines cool coastal cuisine with heat.

Serves 1

INGREDIENTS:
1 tostada
4 1/2 ounces pickled shrimp (approximately 1/4 pound)
1/4 tablespoon raw green sauce
1 teaspoon habanero mayonnaise

PICKLED SHRIMP:
1 1/3 pounds shrimp, diced
1 1/4 cup lime juice, divided
2 teaspoons salt
1/4 teaspoon pepper

RAW GREEN SAUCE:
1 pound tomatillos
2 teaspoons serrano chile
2 tablespoons white onion
1 tablespoon white vinegar
1/2 teaspoon salt plus 1/4 teaspoon, divided
1 pinch of pepper
1 tablespoon cilantro

HABANERO MAYONNAISE:
1 cup mayonnaise
1 habanero chili pepper with seeds
1/2 teaspoon orange zest
Pinch of salt

To pickle the shrimp, combine shrimp, 1 cup lime juice, salt, and pepper in a bowl. Marinate the mixture in the refrigerator for 35 minutes. Remove the excess liquid. Add the additional juice from one quarter of a fresh lime.

Next, make the green sauce. Cut the tomatillos into fourths and place them in the bottom of a blender. Add the rest of the ingredients except the cilantro and blend. Add the cilantro at the end and keep blending.

Finally, make the habanero mayonnaise by blending the plain mayonnaise, habanero chili pepper, and salt in a blender. Incorporate the orange zest at the end.

To assemble, place pickled shrimp on top of the tostada. Top with the green sauce and the mayonnaise.

* * *

ROSARITO *Carlos Acosta & Mauricio Davila*

Carlos Acosta was ready to open a small restaurant in Mexico when he and his cousin and now business partner, Mauricio Davila, then living in San Diego, visited Austin where they found a burgeoning food truck scene and open and eager customers. Changing course and embarking on a mission to "bring a piece of Mexico to Texas," the pair started Rosarito three years ago and have developed enough of a loyal following in that short time to open a second truck this year.

While the first truck continues to focus on the original menu of tacos and burritos, the second introduces more vegetarian and seafood options including tostadas and ceviches. Featuring ingredients like fish, shrimp, octopus, and calamari in raw preparations, the new VW bus still uses the same ingredients and inspiration from Mexico but will be easier to serve from based on simpler food preparation.

While the Austin scene was certainly established in 2014, Rosarito's hand-painted truck became quickly identifiable and developed its customer base through consistent lunch service at office buildings and rotations through breweries like Austin Beer Works, Hops and Grain, and Zilker Brewing. Favorite menu items like the Enchilada Taco and Chiles Rellenos kept customers coming back for more. Eventually, Rosarito built a catering side into the business. Rosarito also became known for its distinctive salsas, ranging from the traditional to spicier combinations like papaya habanero or strawberry habanero with sesame oil. This slight nod to Asian influence is reflected in Acosta's approach to cooking seafood, especially for the steamed rice bowls with tempura fish or shrimp, which became very popular when added in 2015.

Acosta calls his personal favorite menu item, the Governator taco, a "very important taco." It features grilled shrimp with pico de gallo and a cheese chicharron, a creation Acosta came up with himself. Having a hard time finding a good, reasonably priced Mexican cheese, Acosta played around with a few options. Finally, he found one that when burnt brings out a rich flavor. It was an instant hit and signature offering often requested by customers on other dishes including the calamari taco and off menu tacos like the al pastor special.

As they grow, Rosarito hopes to introduce a wider range of Mexican culinary heritage to customers. But in the meantime, once both trucks are up and running, Acosta hopes to marry the two menus into an eventual brick-and-mortar restaurant giving customers the opportunity to combine the offerings between the two trucks into a surf and turf meal.

IT'S ALL GOUDA
Courtesy of Caroline Perini, Easy Slider

Classed-up but still bite size, gouda stars alongside mushrooms and garlic, plus a fancy French garnish.

Serves 1

INGREDIENTS:
10 cloves garlic, peeled
1 cup mayonnaise
3 ounces Angus beef, formed into a patty
Sea salt
Slider bun
1 slice smoked Gouda cheese
Olive oil
1 tablespoon mushrooms, sautéed in olive oil
1 cornichon pickle

MAKE roasted garlic mayonnaise by first roasting peeled garlic cloves seasoned lightly with olive oil until golden brown (approximately 45 minutes in a 375°F oven). Chop the roasted garlic finely and mix with mayonnaise.

Sear one side of the Angus beef patty on a hot griddle. Cook the patty for approximately 3 minutes. Lightly season with sea salt.
Once the patty begins to brown along the edges, use a spatula to flip the beef patty. Use the back and heel of a spatula to press firmly and smash the beef patty into the griddle.

Let the slider rest and cook for approximately 4 more minutes. Meanwhile, toast a slider bun.

Melt half of a slice of smoked Gouda cheese onto the beef patty. Place cooked, beef patty onto the toasted bottom of the slider bun. Use a knife or spreader to spread 1 1/2 teaspoons (or enough to cover the entire bun) of roasted garlic mayonnaise on the top of the toasted slider bun.

Pile approximately 1 tablespoon of the sautéed mushrooms on top of the mayonnaise.

Carefully flip the top bun onto the beef patty ensuring all the ingredients stay together and intact. Garnish with stabbed cornichon pickle.

OLD WORLD KIELBASA SANDWICH
WITH BOURBON GLAZE MUSTARD, APPLE HORSERADISH SLAW, AND SOPHIE'S PIEROGI GARNISH

Courtesy of Stephen Redzinak, Sophie's Gourmet Pierogi

All the flavors of the traditional sausage and pierogi dinner are combined into one glorious sandwich with a few handcrafted condiments to take it over the top.

INGREDIENTS:
Kielbasa sausage (Store or butcher bought. Follow smoking guidelines below if raw.)
Hoagie Roll
Pierogi of your choice, preferably Sophie's Gourmet Pierogi, cooked according to package instructions

BOURBON GLAZE MUSTARD:
1 cup brown sugar
1 tablespoon water
1/2 cup bourbon
2 cups whole grain mustard

APPLE HORSERADISH SLAW:

3 cups green cabbage, finely shredded
2 cups Pink Lady apples, finely julienned or shredded
1 tablespoon lemon juice to prevent apples from browning
1 cup Chinese celery, finely minced or sliced thin (regular celery is ok, leaves and all)
1/4 cup fresh horseradish, finely grated (from a jar is also acceptable)
1 Pink Lady apple, washed, peel on, cored, large dice
1/2 cup apple cider vinegar
1/4 cup honey
1 tablespoon lemon juice
1 teaspoon dry mustard
1 teaspoon granulated onion
1 teaspoon granulated garlic
Salt and pepper, to taste
1/4 cup olive oil of your preference

IF THE KIELBASA is raw, smoke at a low temperature, around 170° to 190°F for 2 to 3 hours or until internal temperature reaches 160°F. Submerge the cooked sausage into ice water to stop the cooking process and keep the casing from shrinking. Remove from water and set out at room temp to allow sausage to bloom for approximately 1 hour. Refrigerate the cooked sausage until ready for use on the sandwich.

To make the mustard, first, simmer brown sugar and water over medium heat until lightly reduced to a syrup. Remove the sauce from the flame and deglaze with the bourbon. Return the sauce back to the flame and reduce the mixture again to a syrup until it is thick enough to coat the back of a spoon. Combine the finished syrup with the mustard to the desired sweetness.

For the slaw, combine all ingredients except oil in a blender, as blender spins slowly add the oil to emulsify, adjust seasoning to taste, and then chill in the refrigerator.

To assemble sandwich, warm the sausage on a grill or griddle, select your favorite hoagie roll, smear the mustard inside the bread, top with two pierogi, and add slaw to finish.

Enjoy with a side of pierogi and a cold glass of beer!

SOPHIE'S GOURMET PIEROGI
Stephen Redzinak

Customers had been asking Stephen Redzinak to package his pierogi since the beginning of Sophie's Gourmet Pierogi, but he was nervous. "It's like handing off your baby to a babysitter," says Redzinak of handing someone his handcrafted product uncooked and trusting them to prepare it as he would on his truck. But when local grocer Weiland's Market reached out asking if he could fill a demand they had for pierogi, Redzinak took it as a sign and made the leap into packaging not only his pierogi but three of his signature compound butters.

Weiland's along with a few other local markets in the area now carry Redzinak's signature potato pierogi. His original goal was to create the best potato-filled pierogis anyone has ever had and to top them with either his lemon basil, roasted garlic smoked paprika, or mustard grain and chive compound butters. Customer response has been encouraging. Selling out of his product each week, Redzinak has expanded Sophie's website (http://www.sophiesgourmet.com) to include information on how to serve the pierogis, inspirations for using them in dishes, and other ways to use the compound butters. Though it's only been a few months, Redzinak sees great growth potential and hopes to one day have a national presence for the packaged offering.

To meet this demand, Redzinak acquired a commissary production kitchen, which in former iterations had served as a florist, a photography studio and a pizza shop. Seeing a brick-and-mortar opportunity, he gained approval from the city of Groveport to open for lunch Monday through Friday. It's kept him even busier through the winter months. The truck will continue to travel around come spring rotating amongst local breweries and taprooms for dinner service featuring beer and pierogi pairings. One such event will be hosted at Blystone Farm in Canal Winchester, a full service butcher shop and deli selling many local products and which recently opened a taproom and restaurant. Redzinak likes playing with out of the ordinary fillings and accompaniments for these events, as well as promoting Blystone's Old World style kielbasi. Redzinak smokes the kielbasi and serves them with pierogi and sauerkraut, a dish he grew up eating at his Grandmother Sophie's house. Since she always served the dish with mustard on the side, he created his mustard grain butter to pay homage to her memory, thus fashioning the perfect combination.

Redzinak also has fun with sandwich specials such as the brisket he served during a pop up dinner at Three Tigers Brewing where he played "restaurant for a day." The now customer favorite cheesesteak he concocted for truck service at Seventh Son Brewery honors his upbringing in New Jersey and his half-Polish half-Puerto Rican heritage. Building a cheesesteak sandwich with a Latin flair got Redzinak's wheels turning, and now he alludes to the potential for a second brand to celebrate the other half of his heritage. Whether he'll name it after another family member remains to be seen.

PB & J BANH MI SANDWICH
Courtesy of Todd Edwards, Ole Latte Food Cart

This recipe was created to stand up against the vast selection of Vietnamese French bread sandwiches and to utilize our wonderful selection of Rose City Pepper Jams. The heat of the peanut butter (we recommend Portland Spicy Peanut Butter) and the jam combine with the textures of fresh vegetables, bringing out the savory notes found in the best peanut butter and jelly sandwiches.

Serves 1
INGREDIENTS:
Onion bagel
1 1/2 ounces spicy peanut butter
Garlic Ginger Rose City Pepper Jam (or similar spicy jam)
1 3-ounce piece of seared ham (optional)
5 leaves sweet large leaf Thai basil
5 to 6 slices cucumber
2 ounces carrots, julienned
1/4 avocado, sliced
Kale (lightly salted and massaged)
Black pepper

THE PB & J BANH MI sandwich starts on a toasted onion bagel (or any other bagel for that matter), and a healthy serving of Portland Spicy Peanut Butter on the topside.

On the opposite (or bottom side) of the bagel, spread the Garlic Ginger Rose City Pepper Jam. Then top the jam with the ham, Thai basil, and cucumbers.

On top of the cucumbers, add a thin layer of carrots and avocado before capping it off with the kale and black pepper.

TRAFFICKING TURKEY
Courtesy of Zach James, Paddy Wagon

A decadent take on a turkey melt. The sweet and hot pepper jelly makes this special.

Serves 1
INGREDIENTS:
1 tablespoon butter
3 slices roasted turkey breast
2 slices sourdough bread
2 tablespoons habanero pepper jelly (store bought or your favorite recipe)
3 slices brie cheese
3 slices bacon, cooked crisp

PREHEAT a griddle or nonstick pan.

Melt the butter in the pan to make buttering the bread easier. Warm the turkey gently in the same pan before proceeding.

For each slice of bread, butter one side and slather pepper jelly on the other.

Lay one slice of bread on a plate, butter side down. Layer 2 slices of brie on top of the pepper jelly. Layer the bacon and turkey on top of the cheese. Finally, place one more slice of brie on top of the turkey and place the remaining bread on top, butter side up.

Place the sandwich on the griddle and cook over medium heat until the bread is golden brown and the brie is melted. Serve immediately.

PADDY WAGON *Zach James*

As both "Sheriff" of Paddy Wagon and President of the Central Ohio Food Truck Association, Zach James quite literally wears multiple hats for his roles in the Columbus mobile food scene. He's grown both personally and professionally since his start on the campus of Ohio State University and now leads both his own business as well as the local industry association serving over seventy members.

With a mission to advocate for food truck owners and mobile food operators serving Central Ohio, COFTA was established to provide a platform for advocacy, communication, and education for members and the community they serve. James's leadership of the group has also allowed them to grow large enough to have their own festival first introduced in 2016.

He's also been growing the Paddy Wagon brand around town, shifting focus away from brick-and-mortar installations or pop ups at local bars, instead to the continued expansion of the mobile fleet. In the last year, he's added two additional mobiles, one truck and one push cart, and has plans to expand operations into the Cleveland and Cincinnati markets by 2019.

While staying true to his original sources of familial inspiration (his mom and grandma's home cooking), James has worked to polish the Paddy Wagon offering deconstructing many of the recipes to make them as much from scratch as possible. This applies especially to his sauces including the habanero pepper jelly, a secret he keeps confidential, only sharing that "the basics of any homemade jelly are included in ours—fresh fruit, peppers (diced), raw sugar, and fruit pectin." Coming from a family that was big on meaty, cheesy dishes, James focuses on "comfort inspired classics," but with his signature twist, and of course, quirky names to play into the Paddy Wagon theme.

Acknowledging that both the greatest challenge and the greatest reward is to simply "keep the wheels turning," James has positioned Paddy Wagon not only to sustain but to evolve bringing his unique brand to a larger audience hungry for favorites like the Trafficking Turkey and Sherriff's Roll, which he shares here.

TREASURE ISLAND ROLL
Courtesy of Alex Naung, Wasabi Sushi PDX

Named while watching the show Las Vegas, Naung remembers seeing the volcano erupt at the Treasure Island Hotel and Casino and made the association with the spicy tuna featured in the roll.

Serves 1

INGREDIENTS:
2 cups short grain sushi rice
3 cups of water
1/2 tablespoon of sushi seasoning vinegar
1/2 ounce mayonnaise
2 ounces crab flakes
1 sheet nori
1/2 teaspoon sesame seeds
1 small cucumber
1 small avocado
1 pound ground tuna
1 teaspoon sesame oil
1 teaspoon salt
2 teaspoon sriracha

SPICY SAUCE:
8 ounces mayonnaise
3 ounces sriracha
1 ounce spicy sesame oil

GARNISH:
1 green onion, sliced
1 ounce masago
Ginger
Wasabi

WASH the rice in several changes of water until the rinse water is no longer cloudy, drain well, and place in the rice cooker. Add 3 cups of water and cook for 45 minutes (30 minutes cooking plus 15 minutes steaming for a total of 45 minutes).

After the rice has cooked, run the rice spatula around the side of the pot and flip the rice out of the container, immediately add sushi seasoning vinegar onto the rice and thoroughly mix the rice and vinegar with the rice paddle for 1 minute. After that, do not cover; allow the rice to rest for 10 minutes, and then mix the rice in a flipping motion to minimize the breaking or smashing of any rice grains. Place rice aside to cool.

Mix the crab flakes with the mayonnaise in a bowl, and set aside.

To roll the sushi, cover a bamboo rolling mat with plastic wrap. Lay a sheet of nori, shiny side down, on the plastic wrap. With wet fingers, firmly pat a thin, even layer of prepared rice over the nori, leaving 1/4-inch uncovered at the bottom edge of the sheet. Sprinkle the rice with about 1/2 teaspoon of sesame seeds, and gently press them into the rice. Carefully flip the nori sheet over so the seaweed side is up.

Place 2 long cucumber spears, 2 or 3 slices of avocado, and about 1 tablespoon of crab salad mixture in a line across the nori sheet about 1/4 from the uncovered edge. Pick up the edge of the bamboo rolling sheet, fold the bottom edge of the sheet up enclosing the filling, and tightly roll the sushi into a cylinder about 1 1/2 inches in diameter. Once the sushi is rolled, wrap it in the mat and gently squeeze to compact it tightly.

Cut each roll into 10 pieces with a very sharp knife dipped in water. Place all of the pieces on a plate.

In a separate bowl, combine ground tuna (make sure to squeeze all of the water out) with 1 teaspoon sesame oil, 1 teaspoon salt, 2 teaspoons sriracha. Mix well to combine, then place mixture on top of the sliced roll, mounding into the shape of a volcano.

Assemble the sauce by combining mayonnaise, sriracha, and spicy sesame oil. Drizzle the the sauce on top of the roll. Garnish with green onion and masago sprinkled on top. Serve with the ginger and wasabi on the side.

WASABI SUSHI PDX *Alex Naung*

First, there was a Sushi Burrito, then came the Sushi Donut, and now, for his fourth location of Wasabi Sushi PDX the always innovative Alex Naung brings fans the Sushi Burger. It may sound crazy to the unfamiliar, even sacrilegious to purists, but to those that have been following Naung's rapid expansion since opening a small food court in November 2015, it's nothing but delicious.

With a varied background from his upbringing in Myanmar (Burma) to stints in London, Hawaii, Phoenix, and finally Portland, Nuang developed his own style after years of working in sushi restaurants. Marrying this style with his desire to start his own business, Naung opened his first location in the Happy Valley area focusing on sushi only wanting to offer a quality product at an affordable price. After only a year in operation, success afforded him the ability to open both a second and third location within days of each other in November 2016. Around the same time, he added his Sushi Burrito named for its playful presentation rather than Mexican ingredients. Shortly after, came the Sushi Donut featuring spicy tuna or crab salad in a donut shape.

Growth continues in 2017 with the opening of the first brick-and-mortar location, a full new construction build-out just for Wasabi Sushi. And next in menu expansion? The Sushi Burger complete with sushi rice molded into a bun and grilled to hold a meatloaf shaped "patty" of spicy tuna, topped with avocado, cucumber, lettuce, and spicy mayonnaise.

Naung has fun creating new items for each new location and loves the reaction he has gotten from customer favorites like the burrito and donut. His personal favorites are the fried items, especially the soft shell crab (which is also offered as a "burger," sandwiched between two rice patties), and then a menu original, the Treasure Island Roll, which he shares here. Other signatures, like the Hawaiian Mango Dragon, pay homage to his previous home and where he got his start in the business. Whether you pick a signature sushi roll, an innovative new favorite, or customize your own creation, Naung ensures you'll experience sushi in a new way, one he hopes to continue to expand to customers nationwide.

THE SEARED AHI TUNA
Courtesy of Caroline Perini, Easy Slider

Branching out from strictly beef, Perini offers a seafood slider that showcases the versatility of the Easy Slider concept, as well as an addictive Asian-Cashew Slaw.

Serves 1

INGREDIENTS:
3 ounces ahi tuna steak
Slider bun, toasted
Olive oil
1/2 cup chili garlic sauce (store bought)
1 cup mayonnaise
Asian-Cashew Slaw
1/2 cup carrots, shredded
1/2 cup red cabbage, shredded
12 snow peas, sliced
2 tablespoons salted cashews, chopped
2 tablespoons rice vinegar
1 lime, cut into wedges

SEAR the ahi tuna steak to medium rare, on either a grill/griddle or pan. Place the tuna onto the slider bun bottom.

To make garlic chili mayonnaise, mix chili garlic sauce with any mayonnaise to taste based on spice preference.

Onto the slider bun top, spread 1 tablespoon (or enough to cover the entire bun) of the garlic-chili mayonnaise.

Assemble the slaw by mixing the shredded carrots, red cabbage, and sliced snow peas in a bowl. Add the chopped, salted cashews and mix in the rice vinegar to taste.

Heap approximately 1 1/2 tablespoons of the slaw on top of the mayonnaise. Serve the slider with a lime wedge.
Flip the top bun onto the tuna, ensuring all ingredients stay together and intact.

Garnish with a stabbed, quarter lime wedge.

SHERRIFF'S ROLL
Courtesy of Zach James, Paddy Wagon

Part hamburger, part hand pie, all delicious.

Serves 8

DOUGH:
3/4 cup warm water
1/2 ounce active dry yeast (2 packets)
4 tablespoons sugar, divided
500 grams all purpose flour (about 4 cups)
1 teaspoon salt
3/4 cup whole milk, room temperature
4 tablespoons unsalted butter, melted, plus two additional tablespoons for brushing at the end

FILLING:
2 pounds ground beef
1/3 cup onion, chopped
2 to 3 ounces grated Cheddar cheese
1 teaspoon Worcestershire sauce
1 teaspoon table salt
1 teaspoon freshly ground pepper

PLACE the yeast and 1 teaspoon of the sugar in the warm water and let it sit for 5 minutes. It should become frothy on top if the yeast is active (if it doesn't, check the date on the packets). In a large bowl, combine the flour, remaining sugar, and the salt. Add the water mixture, the milk, and the melted butter and stir to thoroughly combine. The mixture will be somewhat lumpy and sticky. Place a damp towel over the bowl and allow the dough to rise for 1 hour or until doubled in volume.

Meanwhile, brown the meat and the onion together in a skillet. Remove the mixture from the heat and drain the excess drippings from the meat. Allow the meat to cool to room temperature. Add the cheese, Worcestershire sauce, salt, and pepper and stir to combine. This will be the final flavor of the filling so taste it and adjust the seasoning if needed.

When the dough has risen, remove it to a generously floured surface and knead it until it is no longer sticky, adding flour as is necessary. The goal is to have a ball of dough that is not sticky and that will rebound when you press on it with your finger, so keep adding a pinch of flour here and there, and kneading it, until you achieve the desired result. This should take about 5 to 7 minutes.

Using a floured rolling pin, roll out the dough into a 16 by 16-inch square. Cut the square into 16 square pieces of dough by cutting the dough into 4 columns, and then cutting each column into 4 equal pieces. Each piece should be roughly 4 by 4 inches. Roll each piece until it is slightly larger.

Divide meat mixture into 8 equal scoops, then form each into a fat patty with your hands and place one each on 8 of the dough squares. Cover each patty with another square of dough, and pinch it around the edges to fully seal the pillow that you create. Tuck the edges underneath the pillow and gently pinch the seam into the bottom of the pillow a bit.

Place each burger onto a lightly buttered cookie sheet leaving 2 inches between each burger. Set aside and allow the dough to rise again for 20 minutes until the burgers are puffy and enlarged.

Meanwhile, preheat the oven to 350º F. Once the dough burgers have finished rising their final time, place them in the oven and bake until they are golden brown, about 30 minutes.

Brush the tops with a little melted butter and serve hot with mustard and ketchup on the side.

COLUMBUS FOOD TRUCK CULTURE:

Kevin Brennan and Mike Gallicchio

The Midwest has an incredibly diverse food truck scene that blossomed almost overnight. We asked Kevin and Mike to help describe the vibe of the Columbus food truck culture.

KEVIN BRENNAN, ECDI FOOD FORT, COLUMBUS, OHIO

I've lived in Columbus my entire life, but I didn't really start to follow the mobile food scene until I began working for The Food Fort, a Central Ohio food-based business incubator. I've worked in Columbus's mobile scene for over three years, interacting closely with food truck clients to secure opportunities (procurement, media exposure, business assistance) for them. I've also organized food truck-related events and fundraisers for various companies in Central Ohio.

The food truck scene has taken off in the last few years. The city has embraced the industry by working with food truck advocacy groups, ensuring that Central Ohio is welcoming to those interested in getting into the food truck biz. You can find trucks all over the place—on city streets, at festivals, fundraisers, you name it.

Do you have some pro tips for people visiting the food trucks for the first time?
Be brave and try something new! That's often how I find my new favorite truck. If you're unsure of a menu item, don't be afraid to ask the food truck owner. They are usually excited just by the customer's curiosity in their cuisine.

Which trucks are most reflective of the local culture?
Mikey's Late Night Slice seems like the obvious choice here, as they were the first big mobile success story. They are now featured at nine different locations including local music and event venues as well as brick and mortars throughout the city.

What are the main differences in the food trucks in your city versus other cities?
Other cities seem to have trucks tied to their respective identity. The Northeast coast has their lobster rolls. Southern states tend to focus more towards BBQ. Since Columbus isn't tied to a specific cuisine, it creates more of a diverse trend.

What are some local food trucks that have turned into brick-and-mortar restaurants?
Dos Hermanos Taco Truck now has a permanent stall at the North Market. A lot of food trucks will also pop up in local bars, utilizing their kitchens to sell food specific to their truck's brand. It has created a dynamic atmosphere in the mobile community.

Who are the founding fathers of the food truck revolution in Columbus?
Jim Pashovich, owner of Pitabilities, is known as the godfather of the mobile scene here. He's revolutionized the industry by remaining innovative and exploring new avenues of business; catering, event venue service, etc. He's known by almost all of the food truck owners in the city, and he is always quick to provide advice to those interested in the business. I've learned a lot from him over the years.

Are the local trucks mobile or stationary?
Most are mobile. There are a few stationary trucks that remain successful, but usually, it's due to some sort of synergy established with the businesses that surround them: hungry bar patrons, established followings that are tied to neighborhoods, friends, etc.

MIKE GALLICCHIO, THE COLUMBUS FOOD TRUCK FESTIVAL AND MOBILE FOOD EXPO, COLUMBUS, OHIO

I'm originally from Columbus and got involved with the mobile food scene when I organized the first Food Truck Festival in 2011 at the request of Columbus Commons. The special events coordinator there at the time had worked for me in the bar business and wanted to do an event to bring people down to the newly opened park.

I've managed bars and restaurants for a long time, then got into the food truck world and have been involved, obviously quite heavily, for the last seven years. I've seen the tremendous growth in the scene here in Columbus. I'm not a chef or even a cook, but my current role as co-owner of the annual Columbus Food Truck Festival and the Mobile Food Conference and Expo allows me to know everyone in the industry from a different perspective. I also own the Park Street Festival and Bacon Festival and run the Columbus Commons Food Truck Food Court weekly in the summers. I've also been hired to operate and run other festivals for small towns, which gives me the opportunity to get the street food scene involved in those events.

How are food trucks part of the city's culture?
Our food trucks play a big role, everybody knows them, and there are now iconic brands like Mikey's Pizza, Hot Chicken Takeover, and local favorite Jeni's Splendid Ice Cream, originally a brick and mortar that now has a food truck as well. There are food trucks everywhere including local breweries who frequently host trucks instead of having a kitchen (and we have a lot of breweries in Columbus). The trucks each have their own followings and overall have blended in with our city and environment to become part of the culture.

What is the future of food trucks in Columbus?
I don't see it going anywhere. Some people get out of it, but others are always coming in. It can be a gateway to having a brick and mortar. I've also seen bigger restaurants getting a truck to use as a mobile billboard and then are able to get out to events more. Our scene grew fast because there was little restriction. We have more legislation now, but as long as it's kept in check, the community will continue to grow. Up next, I'd look for fair vendors to move into food trucks. There are people that have been doing festivals for a long time and have six, ten, twelve fair-only units and want to be more mobile.

What are some local food trucks that have turned into brick-and-mortar restaurants?
Challah! had an opportunity to open at Woodlands Tavern. It's part of the progression and natural for growth, but most won't give up their trucks. A lot of people see an opportunity to get into the food business for $50k versus $300k and try it out, then grow to a brick and mortar. It's the American Dream. On the flip side, brands like Greater's Ice Cream, Donato's, and even White Castle have gotten into the scene mainly to do private catering. I think this will continue to happen and get even bigger. They recognize an opportunity, another way to make money and create awareness having a mobile billboard on the freeway. I think everyone should do it and am frankly surprised they haven't—you already have a commissary and staffing (the biggest problem in the mobile food industry).

Who are the founding fathers of the food truck revolution in your city?
Jim Pashovich of Pitabilities, who I truly respect and has been doing this for a long time. Chas Kaplan, my partner and co-founder of the Food Truck Festival. Zach James of Paddy Wagon—I remember when he was a kid with a broken-down food truck on Neil Avenue, and now he's leading the Central Ohio Food Truck Association. Mike Soboro of Mikey's Late Night Slice, he was an original. These guys know the business really well and know everybody. I have respect for the business acumen of the owners of the Cheesy Truck and Angry Wiener who recently bought Mya's Fried Chicken. It has been cool to see them absorb different brands into their mini empire.

What are some keys to success for food truck owners in your city?
Don't grow until you have the right people underneath you. You cannot grow without good people. I share the same sentiment with Columbus legend Woody Hayes: "You win with people." The other thing would be to take your time, look at someone like Jim Pashovich who has shown that patience and a methodical approach to growth ensure success.

What food truck festivals are happening in Columbus and the surrounding area?
Of course, the Columbus Food Truck Festival which is now in its seventh year and moving to a new location at Bicentennial Park. It's a beautiful wide open area with the Center of Science and Industry (COSI) right across the street, lots of parking, and a location that's right between downtown and the Franklinton neighborhood. We're also teaming up with Nationwide Children's Hospital to bring their annual duck race downtown on the same Saturday. We have great bands, live music on two stages, arts and crafts, and local beer. This year, we will have about 65 trucks both from Columbus as well as outer regions (including Cleveland, Akron, Athens, Lancaster, and Dayton), which gives Columbus locals a great opportunity to try different trucks.

MAIN COURSES

BEEF BACON CHEDDAR STUFFED MEATBALLS MANGIAMO HANDMADE STREET FOOD

BRIE STUFFED PIEROGI WITH FRIED CHICKEN, APPLE BUTTER AND ROSEMARY, HONEY & PEPITAS COMPOUND BUTTER SOPHIE'S GOURMET PIEROGI

CARDAMOM CHAI CHICKEN DESIPDX

CIDER BRAISED LOIN CHOPS RAY RAY'S HOG PIT

CHORIZO SUNNYSIDE TACOS

CRISPY UMAMI CHICKEN WINGS THE PEACHED TORTILLA

GREEN CHILE CLAM CHOWDER DOCK & ROLL

GRILLED HIBACHI CHICKEN HAPA RAMEN PDX

GUINNESS BRAISED PULLED PORK MANGIAMO HANDMADE STREET FOOD

HAWAIIAN STYLE AHI LIMU POKE HAPA RAMEN PDX

JUMBOLAYA SWEET T'S SOUTHERN STYLE FOOD TRUCK

LAMB BACON CHALLAH!

LECHON ASADO THE GUAVA TREE TRUCK

MELBOURNE POWER GRAINS BOWL KINETIC

SHRIMP & GRITS SWEET T'S SOUTHERN STYLE FOOD TRUCK

SWEET/SOUR/SPICY CHICKEN WINGS BURGER STEVENS

VALENTINA CEVICHE ROSARITO

BEEF BACON CHEDDAR STUFFED MEATBALLS

Courtesy of Joe Cockerell, Mangiamo Handmade Street Food

I serve these on ciabatta bread with a bacon-bourbon BBQ sauce, but I can't give that one away! Play around with one of your own recipes. Just drink some bourbon and get creative!

Makes approximately 2 dozen

INGREDIENTS:
2 pounds ground beef
Bacon bits (as much as you want)
2 eggs
1 1/2 cups bread crumbs
1 cup parsley
1 tablespoon salt
1 tablespoon pepper
1 teaspoon garlic powder
1 tablespoon Worcestershire sauce
24 cubes cheddar cheese

MIX all ingredients together except for the cheese.

Grease up your tray and preheat oven to 375° F.

Roll the ground beef mixture into golf ball-sized meatballs, then with your thumb make a small well in the middle of each meatball. Take a cube of cheese and place into the well, surround the cheese with the meat mixture and roll back into shape.

Bake in the oven for 30 to 40 minutes or until they have reached the desired temperature.

Mangiamo! (Let's eat!)

MANGIAMO HANDMADE STREET FOOD *Joe Cockerell*

It all started with a meatball. Joe Cockerell made it his goal to perfect his recipe and spent nearly a year on research and development. He posted pictures of his test kitchen results on Facebook for a growing audience that was anxious to try them first hand.

After selling his car to buy a food cart and convincing the owners of India Oak Bar and Grill to let him feed their hungry crowd, Cockerell opened for business on St. Patrick's Day 2016. His offerings that day consisted of not only his meatball and Chicago-style Italian beef, but a holiday appropriate Guinness braised pulled pork, which he shares on page 112.

Though the name "Mangiamo" has Italian roots and translates to "let's eat," it serves more as a rallying cry than a strict limitation for Cockerell's cuisine. He chose it after seeing how much food waste there is in the industry at large and wanting to do something different. Creative uses for leftover ingredients such as turning extra chicken piccata into Italian wedding soup allow Cockerell to do his part and encourage others to do the same.

Mangiamo grew a steady following over the spring and summer months with hits like the bacon beef cheddar meatball created specifically for the 2016 Bacon Festival. Anticipating the winter months, Cockerell teamed up with Savor Growl, a local beer shop, to build out their makeshift kitchen and started serving an expanded menu in October. With the ability to offer flatbreads, soups, and paninis alongside his signature items, a couple of new favorites have emerged including Joe's Favorite Flatbread featuring pepperoni, bacon, capicola and banana peppers, and a trending bar snack favorite, totchos—tator tots covered in chili, queso, sour cream, pico de gallo, and fried jalapeños. Sounds Mexican, not Italian, huh? It might be the inspiration for a second brand, which Cockerell is contemplating based on opportunities for another location. Perhaps he'll name it "Comamos?"

Serves 4

INGREDIENTS:
BRIE STUFFED PIEROGI
(approximately 20 pierogi):

3 cups flour
Salt
Pepper
1/4 cup toasted pepitas (pumpkin seeds), pulsed in the food processor
1 bunch fresh rosemary, pulsed in the food processor
1/2 cup sour cream
1/2 cup water
2 eggs
1 pound brie, cut into small pieces

FRIED CHICKEN:

1 1/2 teaspoons salt
1 1/2 cups flour
1 teaspoon freshly ground black pepper
1/2 teaspoon cayenne pepper
1 cup buttermilk
4 boneless skinless chicken breasts, cut into 8 pieces and slightly pounded out to similar thickness
Vegetable oil

BRIE STUFFED PIEROGI
WITH FRIED CHICKEN, APPLE BUTTER AND ROSEMARY, HONEY & PEPITAS COMPOUND BUTTER

Courtesy of Stephen Redzinak, Sophie's Gourmet Pierogi

Originally conceived for a pop-up dinner, Redzinak was eager to share this creation after receiving rave reviews from that night's crowd.

APPLE BUTTER:
5 1/2 pounds apples, peeled and cored
4 cups white sugar
1/4 teaspoon ground cloves
2 teaspoons ground cinnamon
1/4 teaspoon salt

ROSEMARY, HONEY & PEPITAS COMPOUND BUTTER:
1 pound whipped unsalted butter
1/4 cup honey, or more or less, for desired sweetness
2 tablespoons fresh rosemary, finely minced
2 tablespoons pepitas (pumpkin seeds, toasted and crushed
Pinch kosher salt

START by making pierogi. In a large bowl, mix the flour, salt, pepper, pepitas, and rosemary. Make a well in the center.

In a separate bowl, mix the sour cream, water, and beaten eggs. Pour this mixture into the well of the dry ingredients. Knead the dough for 8 to 10 minutes.

Cover dough and let rest for 2 hours. Roll out the dough and fill with approximately 1 ounce of the brie cheese.

FOR FRIED CHICKEN, combine the salt, flour, black pepper, and cayenne in a large, shallow bowl. Dredge the chicken in the flour mixture, shaking off the excess. Set aside for about 15 minutes. Pour the buttermilk into a second shallow bowl. Dip the chicken in the buttermilk, then again in the flour mixture.

In a heavy-bottomed Dutch oven (preferably cast iron), heat about 4 inches of vegetable oil over medium heat until the temperature registers 360° F.

Carefully place the chicken into the oil using tongs. Add the pieces slowly, so that the temperature does not drop, and work in batches to avoid overcrowding. Fry the chicken until golden brown, turning once, 10 to 20 minutes, depending on the size of the pieces. Check for doneness by piercing the meat; the juices should run clear.

Drain the chicken on paper towels placed on a wire rack. If desired, the cooked chicken can be kept warm in an oven set on low.

To make the compound butter, whip all the ingredients together to combine.

FOR THE APPLE BUTTER, *place the apples in a slow cooker. In a medium bowl, mix the sugar, cinnamon, cloves, and salt. Pour the mixture over the apples in the slow cooker and mix well. Cover and cook on high 1 hour.*

Reduce heat to low and cook 9 to 11 hours occasionally stirring until the mixture is thickened and dark brown. Uncover and continue cooking on low for 1 additional hour. Stir with a whisk, if desired, to increase smoothness.

Spoon the apple butter into sterile containers, cover, and refrigerate or freeze.

Chef's note: prepare apple butter one day in advance.

Boil pierogi in rolling, salted water until they float, approximately 2 to 3 minutes. The pierogi can be cooked ahead if chilled in ice water after boiled. Heat 1 tablespoon of oil or butter in a nonstick pan over medium heat. Slowly brown pierogi and keep warm over low heat.

To plate, spread 2 tablespoons of apple butter on a plate. Place fried chicken on the apple butter and pierogi on top of the chicken. Finish with the compound butter and garnish with pepitas.

CARDAMOM CHAI CHICKEN
Courtesy of Deepak Saxena, DesiPDX

Tea brined, tea steamed, deep fried, tea glazed, and finished with cardamom salt. This dish was inspired by Vietnamese fried and glazed chicken with a uniquely Indian twist. There are a lot of steps, but it's well worth it!

Serves 6
Special equipment needed:
Kitchen scale
Countertop deep fryer or a deep pan
Candy thermometer
Steaming basket or pan

BRINE:
2 1/2 pounds chicken drumsticks (about 12 pieces)
1 quart water
1 ounce kosher salt
4 black tea bags (Assam variety, Lipton's if not available) or 2 tablespoons loose leaf tea

FOR STEAMING:

2 black tea bags or 1 tablespoon loose leaf black tea
2 cups water

CHAI GLAZE:

1 1/2 tablespoons ginger, grated
4 tablespoons coconut sugar (substitute with brown sugar if not available)
1/2 tablespoon crushed chili pepper
2 black tea bags or 1 tablespoon loose leaf black tea
1/2 teaspoon whole black pepper
1 cup water

ADDITIONAL INGREDIENTS:

1 tablespoon coarse grinding salt or kosher salt
1 tablespoon cardamom, outer husk removed
Enough high heat oil (canola or sunflower) to cover one layer of drumsticks

START by brining the chicken. If using tea bags, rip them open to get loose leaf tea. Put water, tea, and salt in a saucepan. Bring to a boil and simmer 10 minutes to make sure the salt is fully dissolved. Let the brine cool to room temperature.

Place the chicken in a large bowl or pot and pour the brine over the chicken. Refrigerate the chicken for 12 to 24 hours. The longer you brine, the stronger the tea flavor.

Next, steam the chicken by putting water and tea in a pot with a steam basket. Bring the water to a boil over high heat, then reduce to medium-high heat. Put the brined and drained chicken in a steam basket and steam with a lid for 15 minutes. Chill the steamed chicken in the refrigerator for up to 3 days.

To make the glaze, bring all the ingredients to a gentle boil. Simmer for 10 minutes and then strain into a bowl.

Next, mix the salt and cardamom in a handheld grinder.

Heat the oil to 375º F. Fry the chicken in small batches for 5 minutes at a time and drain on the paper towels. If using a large pot instead of a deep fryer, make sure to let the temperature come back up to 375º after each batch.

Working in batches of four drumsticks at a time, toss the chicken and 2 tablespoons of the glaze in the frying pan or wok until the glaze caramelizes. This should only take 1 to 2 minutes, watch closely so as not to burn the glaze.

Grind cardamom salt on top of the drumsticks. Turn them over and grind the spices onto the other side.

DESIPDX *Deepak Saxena*

After almost 20 years in the tech industry, Deepak Saxena decided to trade in a cushy desk job for a hot kitchen, tapping into a long-rooted passion for cooking and an opportunity to share the flavors of his Indian heritage.

Saxena first discovered a love for cooking for others while in college when a friend asked him to cook a few Indian dishes for fellow roommates and friends. Using his mother's recipe book, he made a half dozen different dishes and left behind the days of boxed mac and cheese to explore the cuisine he'd grown up eating. He says, "Every once in awhile I cook something, and I have this moment of 'this is how mom's cooking tasted!'"

Two of his favorite recipes, which he still requests every time he visits his mom are her spicy catfish and khadi (buttermilk yogurt curry) both served with a side of sautéed kale and coriander seeds. Saxena finds the current obsession with kale somewhat amusing having grown up eating it. He says, "Both of these dishes were just popping with strong pungent flavors, and that pungency is something I am working on slowly adding to my menu, as I don't think it is something people are as used to here."

While he's lived everywhere from India to Mozambique, Brazil to Indiana, and Phoenix to Portland, he believes all of these places have affected him in some way. Portland specifically matches his values of individual creativity over mass-produced culture. Saxena says that Portland resembles a "small city trying to be big and at the same time a big city trying to stay small. The most defining aspect about Portland is our sense of place. People have a deep connection to our geography of the mountains and the ocean at a larger scale and a strong sense of our neighborhoods at the small scale." This manifests in ways like an ever-growing number of breweries and coffee shops focused on serving residents, bike lanes, and even an urban growth boundary that protects farms. Saxena uses the term "ethical decadence" to describe the lifestyle joking, "We love our booze, our coffee, our donuts, our strippers, but we want to make sure that they are all organic and fair trade."

Since opening in April 2015, DesiPDX has been continuously listed on Eater's best food cart list and receives high reviews on Yelp in large part to customer favorite the Cardamom Chai Chicken. The dish features chicken drumsticks that are brined in tea overnight, steamed with tea, deep fried, glazed with a chai glaze and then finished with fresh ground cardamom and salt.

For his personal favorite, Saxena recommends the Masala belly. This dish features pork belly that he brines in tamarind and ginger for seven days and then braises for twelve hours on top of onions. Saxena says, "The onions get caramelized, the pork belly is melt in your mouth, and this is all topped with deep-fried chickpeas that offer a nice crunch to balance out the textures. This is my usual meal at the food cart with a bit of rice and my spicy cabbage slaw."

With a focus on farm to cart dining, Saxena feels honored to work with so many farms and says it gives him a sense of participating in something bigger than just his food cart. He has also built strong relationships with many regular customers and their families, including an eight-year-old customer who always asks for DesiPDX when he returns from vacation. Saxena is excited about that opportunity to connect and driven by the desire to feed people not just a plate of food but to give them a nourishing experience.

CIDER BRAISED LOIN CHOPS
Courtesy of James Anderson, Ray Ray's Hog Pit

After I started raising my own heritage breed hogs, I started making a lot of loin chops, and this is my favorite way to do them.

Serves 4

INGREDIENTS:
4 1-inch chops
2 tablespoons salt
1 tablespoon black pepper
3 tablespoons olive oil
1 quart apple cider
1 cup apple cider vinegar
3 tablespoons cornstarch
1/2 cup cold water
3 lemons
Fresh flat leaf parsley

PREHEAT a skillet with olive oil over medium heat.

Coat the chops, top and bottom, with the salt and pepper.

Put the chops in the pan and sear the outside for 3 minutes until medium to dark brown in color. Flip the chops and repeat on the other side.

Place the seared chops into an oven safe dish in a single layer. Add the apple cider and the apple cider vinegar. Cover and cook in the oven at 225º F for 3 hours. The chops should be very tender (easily cut with a fork), if they are not, let them cook for additional time checking them every hour.

Remove the chops from the braising liquid and pour the braising liquid into a small sauce pot and heat the liquid over medium-high heat.

In a small bowl, blend the cornstarch and cold water to make a slurry, and slowly whisk the slurry into the braising liquid until you have a pan jus, which is like a thinner gravy. Taste the pan jus and add salt and pepper if needed. The sauce will need to come to a bubble to reach its full thickness. Pour the pan jus over the chops, squeeze a lemon over the top, and use the remaining lemons for garnish. Top with chopped fresh parsley.

* * *

RAY RAY'S HOG PIT *James "Ray Ray" Anderson*

After five years of focusing on serving the best barbecue possible to the always long line formed outside of his iconic Columbus food truck, James "Ray Ray" Anderson was hungry for more wanting to further his expertise in the barbecue trade and become part of the full process. So he decided to take things to the next level starting his own pig farm in nearby Granville.

Anderson Farms fulfills his goal of becoming more well-rounded and has allowed him to raise pigs of many varieties giving him different flavor profiles of pork to cook with. Since starting the farm in 2014, Anderson has grown the farm to 150 head of swine made up of breeds including the common variety Red Wattle and Large Black to the coveted Berkshire, Duroc and Mangalista and even the rare Poland China and Mulefoot, which he loves for its deep red color that looks like beefsteak.

Anderson says that most Americans are used to the pink Yorkshire pig, which is traditionally farmed for mass consumption meaning farmers are compensated for meat over fat. He prefers to raise his hogs the old fashioned way, allowing the fat and marbling to become pronounced and even cooking the meat with the fat on. By pasture raising his pigs, he can control the fat, richness, size, what they eat, and how long they grow.

High-end chefs in the area appreciate this level of dedication. Anderson Farms has been supplying to A&R Group, which operates the Crest, Market Italian Village, and the kitchen at Hoof Hearted Brewing and chefs like Bill Glover of Gallerie Bar & Bistro at the Hilton and Seth Lassak of Wolf's Ridge Brewing.

While the farm can't quite keep up with the quantity demanded for his food truck just yet, Anderson has been using some of the heritage product for the rotating Saturday specials, including his Whole Hog Sandwich. Instead of cooking the pig in its entirety, he breaks it down and cooks the pork in pieces from the ham to the loin and the belly, and then shreds them up and mixes together to be served. Other Saturday specials that have become favorites include the Mofongo sandwich, a creation by established Columbus Chef Dan Varga, and the BBQ Brisket Philly, which features a beer cheese sauce based on a beer from Jackie O's, a brewpub in Athens, Ohio.

While the truck continues to do what it does best, the farm has recently expanded to open its doors to visitors, especially for weddings. Anderson says they "love to share what we do" and after recently remodeling the 1900s-era barn into an event space, they "dream of having country folk come here and get married out in the pasture with our pergola, hay bales and livestock in the background."

CHORIZO *Courtesy of Joshua Di Bari, Sunnyside Tacos*

Once made, this versatile protein can be featured in a multitude of dishes, from nachos to quesadillas and tacos or combined with potatoes for a hash (page 27). With the proper equipment and hog casings, one could even make individual sausages.

Makes roughly 5 1/2 to 6 pounds

INGREDIENTS:

1 poblano pepper
2 jalapeño peppers
1 medium onion
4 cloves garlic
5 pounds pork shoulder (at least 30% fat)
2 1/4 tablespoons kosher salt
1 tablespoon paprika
1 1/2 teaspoons cracked black pepper
1 1/2 teaspoons onion powder
1 1/2 teaspoons garlic powder
1 tablespoon chili powder
1 1/2 teaspoons ground cumin
3/4 teaspoon dried oregano
1 1/2 teaspoons chili flake (more if desired)
1 bunch of parsley and cilantro
3 tablespoons honey
2 tablespoons of hot sauce (preferably Valentina)
4 ounces white wine or water
6 whole dried ancho chilies or other dried peppers of your choice

FIRST, dice all of the fresh vegetables: peppers, onion and garlic; they don't have to be pretty. To cut back on the level of spice, remove the seeds from the peppers if you wish. After they are chopped, place them in a heavy pan and sauté over low to medium heat until they are translucent, soft, and tender (approximately 6 minutes). Place the cooked mixture on a cookie sheet or large plate and refrigerate.

While that is cooling, dice the pork shoulder and place in the refrigerator or freezer. While the raw meat and vegetables are chilling, portion the rest of your ingredients (all the spices can be put in one container, take the herbs and chiffonade them with a sharp knife, so they don't bruise and set aside). Put honey, hot sauce, water or wine, and dried peppers in a blender and blend until very smooth; then blend them a for a few additional seconds. You should have a bright red liquid. Place this mixture in the refrigerator.

Grinding the meat is best accomplished by working fast and clean. Keep everything as cold as possible. If you have space, place the grinding equipment in the freezer to keep it cold before use. Take the diced pork, mix it with the chilled cooked veggies, and grind them with a meat grinder through a medium die; if casing is being used, then case the sausage and grind the mixture twice. Place the ground mixture in a large bowl or a stand mixer (or use your hand and a wooden spoon), mix the meat together with all the spices, fresh herbs, and the cold, bright red liquid. In the event the ground mixture starts to warm, place it back in the freezer for 10 minutes before continuing to work with it. The mixture should be emulsified to the point where it can be picked up by hand and when the hand is turned upside down, the mixture should remain on the hand without falling off. When the mixture has reached this consistency, place a spoonful in a frying pan and cook it to 150º F (internally), let it cool. Add salt and spices to taste.

The completed chorizo can be frozen.

Chef's Note: It is important to work clean, fast, and keep everything cold when making chorizo. A local butcher can grind the meat if necessary, and then the veggies can be finely chopped by hand or in a food processor in lieu of grinding them. If visiting a butcher, tell them the meat is for sausage so they can incorporate parts with high fat content such as the back fat or belly if the shoulder is too lean on its own.

CRISPY UMAMI CHICKEN WINGS
Courtesy of Eric Silverstein, The Peached Tortilla

The crispy umami chicken wings are a signature dish from The Peached Tortilla that represents the fusion of the Asian/Southern-style cuisine perfectly. Makes 25 marinated wings.

Serves 4 to 6

INGREDIENTS:
5 pounds chicken wings
1 cup fish sauce
1/4 cup rice wine vinegar
1/2 cup sugar
1 cup water
2 tablespoons lime juice
2 tablespoons chili garlic sauce
6 cloves garlic

SAUCE (makes 4 ounces):
1 1/2 cups fish sauce
9 cloves garlic
1 small knob of ginger, peeled
3/4 cup honey
1/3 cup rice vinegar
1/3 cup sriracha
3 1/2 teaspoons lime juice, fresh squeezed
2 1/2 cups rice flour
1 ounce either cilantro, mint or Thai basil (hand torn), to garnish

BLEND the fish sauce, rice vinegar, sugar, water, lime juice, chili garlic and garlic in a blender. Place the chicken wings and marinade in a zip top bag and marinate overnight.

For the sauce, place all the ingredients into a blender and blend.

Lightly toss the marinated chicken wings in the rice flour.

Set deep fryer to 350º F and deep fry for 3 1/2 to 4 minutes.

Place chicken wings on a drying rack to let the excess oil run off. Toss the chicken wings in the wing sauce and top with the garnish.

THE PEACHED TORTILLA *Eric Silverstein*

An Austin favorite for seven years now, The Peached Tortilla has grown and evolved dramatically since its start as a leased food truck based out of Pflugerville, Texas, a 35-minute trek from Austin. What started as a 3 or 4-man operation has staffed up to 50 employees in this short time. The operation now consists of two trucks, a brick-and-mortar restaurant that opened in 2014, and the beautiful Peached Tortilla Social House—an event venue and commissary hub for the catering business.

With a street to table mentality, the fast casual restaurant serves the greatest hits from the food truck alongside a new menu of Asian comfort food. The format lends itself to a more plated experience including servers and a cocktail program. Favorites include the Southern Fun, a riff on Chow Fun (a classic Cantonese dish made from stir-frying beef and wide flat rice noodles), the Laksa Bowl, a unique fried rice with Chinese sausage, and specials like Ramen Night. Truck favorite tacos are still a big seller as well from the banh mi to the pad Thai and the Texas classic BBQ brisket. The Social House pulls from

both menus and the catering business, which boasts sous vide hanger steak, ginger soy salmon, Korean braised short ribs and addictive Brussel sprouts.

Owner Eric Silverstein says the restaurant items he spent a lot of time developing hit particularly close to home as they are things he grew up eating, like Hainan chicken and rice, pork belly buns, and the crispy umami chicken wings he shares here.

Silverstein has seen a lot as the business expanded and has a focused eye for continued growth opportunities in a notably saturated Austin restaurant market. He says diversifying the business model has been key. A misperception that food trucks have low overhead (which isn't true) and additional factors such as mechanical issues cause stress on operations. With a lower ceiling for revenue based on volume than a restaurant, the pricing model can be challenging for mobile operators. This has led to trucks focusing on private events and festivals in the summer with pop-up appearances limited to the slower season. But the trucks still serve as a beacon for what the brand stands for and aren't going anywhere. As the The Peached Tortilla continues to help educate customers and pave the way for other mobile operators, look for new outposts and potential partnerships.

GREEN CHILE CLAM CHOWDER
Courtesy of Lee Krassner, Dock & Roll

This is a super fun soup to make on a chilly day or because I am such a soup lover, on any day! We run it primarily as a special during the wintertime, and it is a big hit with the Texas folks. It is a pretty traditional chowder recipe, but we add the zest of New Mexico green chiles to add some flavor and Southwestern flair. In our kitchen, we use fresh clams, but for ease of home preparation, we substituted canned clams as they are much easier to work with. Hope you enjoy making this and sharing it with your friends and family!

Serves 4

INGREDIENTS:
3 bottles clam juice
1 pound Yukon gold potatoes, cut into 1/2-inch pieces
3 tablespoons butter
2 slices bacon, finely chopped
1 onion, chopped into 1/4-inch pieces
3 garlic cloves
2 large stalks celery
Salt and pepper
2 tablespoons all-purpose flour
2 cups seafood stock
6 cans (6 1/2 ounces each) chopped clams, drained, reserve juice
1 bay leaf
1/2 cup heavy cream
1 tablespoon of your favorite hot sauce
1/2 cup Anaheim chile purée (recipe below)

ANAHEIM CHILE PURÉE (makes about 1 cup):
1 Anaheim chile
1 teaspoon blended oil, or your favorite roasting oil
1/2 cup seafood stock
Salt
Pepper

GARNISH:
Paprika
1/4 cup roasted corn kernels off the cob
Chives, chopped
Salt
Pepper

FIRST make Anaheim chile purée. Preheat the oven to 425º F. Place the chile on a sheet tray covered with foil, rub oil on the chile, and season lightly with salt and pepper. Put the chile in the oven to roast until skin is mostly blistered and black, about 8 to 10 minutes. Remove the chile from the oven and use the foil to enclose the chile and let it steam in the refrigerator for at least 10 minutes.

When the chile is cool enough to handle, remove from the foil, put on a glove and use your hands to remove the charred skin. When all the skin is removed, cut the top off the chile and remove the seeds.

Place the chile in the blender with the seafood stock and a pinch of salt and pepper. Blend for 15 to 30 seconds, then strain purée through a fine mesh strainer. Purée will keep in the refrigerator for up to 5 days.

Next, prepare the soup base by bringing bottled clam juice and potatoes to boil in a large saucepan over high heat. Reduce the heat to medium low and simmer until the potatoes are tender, approximately 10 minutes. Remove the base from the heat and reserve.

Melt the butter in a large pot over medium heat. Add the bacon and cook until the bacon browns and is crisp, approximately 6 to 7 minutes. Remove the bacon from the pan and reserve. Add the onions, garlic, and celery with a couple pinches of salt and pepper, and cook until the vegetables soften and the onions are nearly translucent, about 5 to 7 minutes.

Add the flour and stir with a whisk to remove any lumps, and cook flour/vegetable mixture for about 1 minute. Then, add the seafood stock slowly, stirring with a whisk to avoid lumps. When all the stock is in the pot, add the reserved juice from the clams and the bay leaf, then turn the heat up to high until the liquid boils. Turn the heat down to medium low and simmer the soup for about 20 minutes.

Add the potato mixture, reserved clams, cream, Anaheim chile purée, and hot sauce. Simmer for an additional 7 to 8 minutes to let the flavors blend, and stir frequently. Taste the soup and add additional salt and pepper as necessary.

To serve: Sprinkle a touch of paprika, a few pieces of the crispy reserved bacon, roasted corn kernels, and chopped chives around the top of the soup for a nice presentation and a little extra flavor.

Chef's Note: I find this soup (and all soups for that matter) is best if you can make it one day ahead of time, and let it sit overnight in the refrigerator to let all the flavors get to know each other. You will notice the flavor will enhance dramatically. To reheat, bring the soup to a simmer in a pot before serving.

* * *

DOCK & ROLL *Lee Krassner*

It all started with a classic New England-style lobster roll. Wanting to marry a traditional, high-quality product with a more casual and affordable atmosphere and presentation, Lee Krassner started Dock & Roll with the lobster roll alongside a few other items for non-seafood lovers. But it was that lobster roll that quickly garnered both local and national attention, receiving a litany of accolades including Yahoo's Top 10 Most Mouthwatering Lobster Rolls in America and Zagat's Top 5 Must-Try Lobster Rolls in Austin among others. The recognition culminated in a feature on Cooking Channel's *Eat Street* in 2013/14.

Krassner was one of the first to put bacon on a lobster roll, and for The Real BLT he doesn't use just any bacon but his signature chicken fried bacon. Then there's the Guac Lobster, a mash-up featuring the lightly breaded chicken fried bacon as a chip in addition to standard tortilla chips. Branching out from New England, the Shrimp Po Boy pays homage to the Louisiana area with a Creole mustard remoulade that is also served alongside the Crab Croquette special.

The key to Krassner's menu is freshness. He pivoted the concept slightly to reach out with a more encompassing coastal comfort food theme incorporating items from both coasts. For example, the Fish Wich (fried fish sandwich) is reminiscent of a Northeastern-style sandwich with tartar sauce, lemon, and scallion while the fish tacos are a West Coast "flavor party" made up of mahi mahi marinated in a pineapple soy sauce mixture, topped with spicy pineapple slaw, pickled red onion, and cilantro.

New favorites include fried shrimp and fish baskets like the Fish n' Dips featuring 2 to 3 types of homemade tartar sauce offerings, including a spicy version.

Early fans may miss the weird Austin lobster rolls such as the Ninja, Buddha, and Fat Tuesday—a po'boy meets lobster roll hybrid featuring slaw from the shrimp po'boy, roasted corn, and chicken fried bacon all dressed in the Creole mustard remoulade. But never fear, while these classics may no longer appear on the printed menu, they're still available as secret orders, perhaps making them even weirder.

The fleet has expanded from Dock & Roll's original Airstream trailer to include a refurbished trailer both with permanent locations at two different bar and food parks. A third fully mobile food truck can often be found at office lunch services and breweries. Krassner is hopeful the next step will be a brick-and-mortar building though Austin real estate prices are at odds with his goal of trying to make seafood less prohibitively expensive so people can enjoy it multiple times per week. The menu evolution also embraces this philosophy, offering lower priced items that customers can enjoy with greater frequency than the lobster roll, which might be considered a special treat.

Krassner credits passion for the concept and a good reputation around town as the driving forces that keep Dock & Roll moving in the right direction. He says that he's "very thankful to the Austin community to still be around," noting that the "mobile food game is not an easy one, and we want the community to know we're very thankful for their patronage and continuing to support our growth."

GRILLED HIBACHI CHICKEN
Courtesy of Sarah Littman, Hapa Ramen PDX

A quick cook on the grill seals in this flavorful marinade. We like serving it alongside short grain rice.

Serves 8 to 10

INGREDIENTS:
5 pounds boneless, skinless chicken thighs
2 cups shoyu (Japanese soy sauce)
2 cups mirin
1/2 cup sesame oil
1/2 cup brown sugar
10 cloves garlic, crushed
2 teaspoons fresh ginger, grated
Chili flakes, to taste

MIX all the ingredients together and marinate the chicken for 2 hours.

Remove the chicken from marinade and grill for 5 minutes on each side, giving the chicken a crisp exterior while not overcooking it.

* * *

HAPA RAMEN PDX *Michael and Sarah Littman*

The poke craze that's taking the nation by storm is nothing new to Oahu, Hawaii natives Michael and Sarah Littman who grew up with the dish. Poke is served for breakfast, lunch, and dinner in Hawaii and grocery stores even sell it. They're happy to share their take on it with the busy Portland lunch crowd at the original Hapa Ramen PDX cart, now located downtown. Michael says, "It's a healthy dish, one you feel good after eating, which we always did after surfing at the beach."

Poke means "to cut things up" the dish serves to truly highlight the fish as seen in the recipe he shares here.

The Littman's have shared the food of their upbringing with Portlanders since 2013 and capitalized on the opportunity to be the first cart at the creative pod, Tidbit, which opened in August 2014. Though this location is technically their second spot, it is larger in both size and menu. Here the focus is ramen, from the top selling Tonkotsu (the most famous ramen in the world made with a rich, smoky-flavored pork broth) to their signature the G Special (a spicy pork belly broth with lots of toppings including shitake mushrooms, spinach, eggs, and bean sprouts named after it's creator, Sarah's brother). It's the most expensive menu item, but it always sells out.

Personally, Michael favors Tsukamen, a dipping-style ramen where the noodles and broth are separate. Traditionally, this dish is meant to be eaten quickly and while standing, dipping the noodles into the rich broth like a sauce. Sarah's top choice is even more personal. A visiting authentic Japanese ramen guru taught her the recipe for Shoyu—Tokyo-style ramen with a clear broth that acts as a "double soup" combining fish stock and a chicken and vegetable-based broth for complexity. She doesn't speak Japanese, so Michael had to translate for her during the lesson making it a memorable experience for both of them.

The pair loves Portland for its great landscape including trees and mountains, perfect for their love of outdoor activities like hiking and surfing. Michael says it's "family oriented, without a lot of flash, down to earth." He also says that Portlanders are "really interested in food culture and have a huge curiosity about new, interesting, ethnic foods." Most importantly, they "love noodles and the ramen concept is weatherproof because you crave it even in cold weather."

Expansion continues for the couple with the opening of Aiko Ramen, their first brick-and-mortar restaurant located downtown in the new Portland Food Hall. They named the restaurant Aiko (which translates to love) after both the couple's daughter and Michael's grandmother as the restaurant is a celebration of ramen and those who love it as much as they do.

GUINNESS BRAISED PULLED PORK
Courtesy of Joe Cockerell, Mangiamo Handmade Street Food

Delicious in many applications, Cockerell serves his with coleslaw, golden BBQ sauce and fried jalapeños on a brioche bun.

Serves 4 to 6

INGREDIENTS:

1 pork butt (approximately 4 to 5 pounds, boneless or bone in)
1 large white onion, sliced into 1/4-inch pieces
1 tablespoon salt
1 tablespoon pepper
1 tablespoon chili powder
1 tablespoon garlic powder
1 tablespoon paprika
1 tablespoon cinnamon sugar (store bought or made by combining 1/2 cup sugar with 2 tablespoons ground cinnamon)
2 Guinness beers (substitute hard cider, a gluten-free version)

MIX all the spices together.

Score the fat on the pork.

Rub the pork with your seasoning mixture. Be sure to rub it all over the meat and really massage it into the pork. Then wrap in plastic wrap and let it sit refrigerated for at least 2 hours or overnight. Open one of the beers and start drinking it.

Line the bottom of your crock pot with the onions and set it on low for 10 hours. Place the pork on top of the onions fat side down. Pour the other beer on top of the pork and cook on low for 10 hours. If roasting the pork in the oven, set the temperature to 210° F and cook for 9 hours.

Transfer the roasted pork to a baking sheet to let it cool for 10 to 15 minutes. Once cooled slightly, get two forks and shred the meat for serving or use in another recipe.

HAWAIIAN STYLE AHI LIMU POKE
Courtesy of Michael Littman, Hapa Ramen PDX

Poke has finally caught the attention of mainland diners from new restaurants dedicated to the Hawaiian classic to its recent showcase on the cover of Bon Appetit magazine.

Serves 2 to 4

INGREDIENTS:
1 pound of sashimi grade ahi tuna
3 to 4 cloves garlic
1 teaspoon fresh ginger
1/4 cup ogo* (or limu) seaweed
1 1/2 teaspoons of Hawaiian sea salt
Red chili flakes
1 1/2 teaspoons sesame oil
1/2 teaspoon kukui nut oil**
1/2 Maui sweet onion, sliced into desired thickness
Shoyu, as desired
1/4 green onion, sliced

BEGIN by cutting the tuna into 1/2-inch cubes. Mince (do not grate) the garlic and ginger. Chop the ogo into 1-inch pieces. Combine in a bowl.

Add the Hawaiian salt and a sprinkle of red chili flakes, then the sesame and kukui nut oils. Mix the ingredients by hand so that the salt and oils have blended with the fish.

Taste and adjust the oil and salt as necessary, add onion and shoyu, if desired.

Top with fresh cut green onions and serve over rice or greens.

Notes:
Ogo is the seaweed "most likely to show up in your poke. The most popular type is reddish brown, with lacy, branching tendrils that snap under your teeth and taste like the ocean. You might come across ogo in green or light brownish colors, with thicker branches and a slightly heftier bite, too," according to Bon Appetit magazine.

** Kukui nut oil has been used for a long time throughout the islands of Hawaii. Available on Amazon.com.

JUMBOLAYA
Courtesy of Travis Hyde, Sweet T's Southern Style Food Truck

This is a combination of two traditional dishes, Jambalaya and Gumbo.

Serves 4

INGREDIENTS:
1/4 cup flour
1/4 cup butter
2 to 3 tablespoons blended oil
2 green bell peppers, deseeded and diced
2 large Vidalia onions, diced
3 large stalks celery, diced
2 tablespoons garlic, minced
1 tablespoon gumbo filé powder
1 pound chicken thighs, cubed
1/2 pound boneless, skinless chicken breast, cubed
1/2 pound Andouille sausage, diced
2 large tomatoes, diced
8 cups chicken stock
4 cups steamed rice
1/2 cup scallions, sliced

SPICE BLEND:
1 tablespoon cayenne
1 1/2 tablespoons granulated garlic
1 1/2 tablespoons granulation onion
1 tablespoon dried basil
2 teaspoons dried oregano

FIRST make the dark roux (note: this will be the most time-consuming part). Melt the butter in a pan with the flour and cook over medium-low heat, stirring with a wooden spoon until the mixture has completely toasted and has taken on the color of milk chocolate. This will take at least 45 minutes.

Next make the spice blend, combining cayenne, garlic, onion, basil, and oregano.

In a separate medium pot, add a couple of tablespoons of blended oil and add the peppers, onions, celery, and garlic and begin to sauté on medium high heat for a couple minutes. Next, add the roux followed by the filé powder, stirring to coat evenly before adding the chicken and spice blend.

Mix everything together and sauté the chicken for a couple minutes before adding the sausage.

Finally, add the chicken stock and tomatoes and allow this to simmer on medium heat for at least 30 minutes making sure to stir every couple of minutes to prevent food particles from sticking to the bottom of the pan.

Check the seasoning for taste and do not forget to add salt. It should have a slightly thickened consistency, enough to coat a spoon.

To serve, ladle a serving over rice and top with scallions.

For more zip add a little hot sauce or a lot.

Notes:
Blended oil is a blend of 75% extra virgin olive oil and 25% vegetable oil.
Fílé powder is ground sassafras root and it can be bought in most grocery store spice aisles and online as well.

SWEET T'S SOUTHERN STYLE FOOD TRUCK
Travis Hyde

Though a Columbus resident since before middle school, Travis Hyde's roots run south, from West Virginia to the Carolinas and into Louisiana. His extended family of great "from scratch" cooks was helmed by his grandmother whom Travis remembers always had a pot of gumbo on the stove.

He got his start in professional kitchens at just 14 bussing tables at a then popular Italian restaurant, the Monte Carlo. When the chef caught him constantly staring at the cooks, he gave him a chance at garde manger (or keeper of the chilled dishes), and so began a trajectory through some of the city's best restaurants, like Alana's and Z Cucina. While Hyde says he had always loved cooking though never considered it as a career, he became "addicted to the industry and addicted to food" in the most positive sense—a true hunger to constantly evolve and explore new techniques and products. It paid off, as he was honored as WOSU's Chef in the City five times and his braised pork cheek ragu with gnocchi was featured in the Restaurant Hospitality Best Chefs America Cookbook.

With a focus on opening a brick-and-mortar location, Hyde says he "never in a million years" thought he'd be doing a food truck, but managing the kitchen finances in his last two roles, his experience working with accountants, lawyers, licensing, and permitting agents led him to explore the opportunity. Excited about the ability to try out a smaller venue, build a brand, and make a name for himself, Hyde also liked the idea of paying homage to both his and his wife's Southern ties. But it was his young daughter who sealed the deal and ultimately gave the truck its name when she remarked, "You're a sweet chef, you should just be Sweet T."

Representing Southern food with Hyde's own twist, a quick customer favorite has become the bourbon chicken. With a flavorful combination of brown sugar, soy, and ginger, it's often a sell out dish. Hyde's personal favorite, the Shrimp & Grits, is a standout example of slow and low cooking using properly prepared roux (with bacon he smokes himself) and rich and creamy grits.

The menu extends to snacks like Hominy Fries and Fried Green Tomatoes to po'boy sandwiches served on local favorite Matija Bread. From two family recipes, Grandma's gumbo and a jambalaya dish, Hyde created his Jumbolaya which he shares here.

Operating since May 2016, Hyde's food truck has led him to explore a different facet of the industry, but he is still working to open a brick-and-mortar restaurant hopefully sometime in 2018 though he intends to keep the truck, too.

Hyde seems to have found the same love for Columbus as his parents did years ago, saying it's "fast growing and diverse, getting better each year." But while he has put down new roots, both business and family wise, he and his wife still dream of living back down South, perhaps after their son and daughter are grown. For now, Sweet T's delivers on the spirit of Southern hospitality welcoming and showing appreciation through food, the classic way to anyone's heart.

LAMB BACON
Courtesy of Catie Randazzo, Challah!

Not your grocery store packaged bacon, the spice rub enhances the flavor of the lamb, especially after smoking.

Makes roughly 25 pieces of bacon, depending on how thick one slices it.

INGREDIENTS:
5 tablespoons kosher salt
2 teaspoons pink curing salt
3 tablespoons dark brown sugar, packed
4 dried bay leaves, crushed
1 tablespoon plus 1 teaspoon black pepper, freshly ground
1 clove garlic, minced
2 arbol chiles, ground
1 teaspoon cinnamon
1 1/2 to 2 pounds boneless lamb breast with silver skin (connective tissue) intact

COMBINE the salts, brown sugar, bay leaves, and additional spices in a bowl and transfer to a large plate or a baking dish. Dredge the lamb breast in the rub and massage it into the surface of the lamb. (You will probably have some rub left over.) Shake off any excess rub and let the meat sit covered in the refrigerator for 5 days, turning the lamb over once a day.

After 5 days, rinse the lamb thoroughly, pat it dry with paper towels, and allow it to sit uncovered in the refrigerator overnight.

Soak woodchips in water for 30 minutes, then drain and pat them dry. When the temperature inside the smoker has reached 200° F, and the wood chips are smoking steadily, add the lamb and let smoke. This will take about 2 to 3 hours: make sure the temperature is maintained at 200° F, and the lamb reads at a temperature of 160° F when finished. If you do not have a smoker, preheat the oven to 200° F and cook for 2 hours.

CHALLAH! *Catie Randazzo*

Perhaps Catie Randazzo gets her love of unique combinations from her dad, the original creator of Honey Nut Cheerio Pancakes, just one of his Saturday morning pancake specialties. Or maybe her pull into the restaurant world was inspired by visits to the race track in Akron where her aunt was a server for over 30 years—the feeling of knowing someone on the inside making her feel like she was a big deal, getting "hooked up." But more likely it was growing up in a "from scratch" cooking environment where the Sunday sauce started right after the last bite of Saturday pancakes and birthdays were celebrated with apple pies from a recipe passed down by five generations of women, and a "living off the land" ethos that included fall canning in preparation for the long Ohio winter.

After leaving Ohio to cook in both Portland, Oregon and New York City (most recently as chef of Allswell in Brooklyn), Randazzo returned home to be closer to her support system, friends, and family. She missed a few of her favorite culinary go-tos like the family friendly Planks Beer Garden, which brings back childhood memories of her dad pulling her around in a red wagon jokingly yelling, "Kids for sale." Or for a date night, The Rossi where fellow chef and friend Matthew Heaggans "never disappoints." Randazzo also suggests Skillet and Pistacia Vera in German Village, Momo Ghar for ethnic cuisine featuring dumplings, and a beer stop at her second home, Seventh Son Brewery (where you'll also often find Challah! for Sunday brunch service).

If you can't wait for brunch, head over to her new permanent outpost, a kitchen takeover at Woodland's Tavern in Grandview. The Crispy Chicken Sandwich is such a fan favorite that Randazzo ran a contest in which the winner received a free sandwich each week for a year to commemorate the grand opening of the new spot. She jokes that it's the "least "Jew'ish" thing on the menu and offers her personal favorite, The Jewbano, her version of a Cuban but with pastrami and corned beef instead of pork.

Columbus has welcomed Randazzo back with open arms and embraced her food since opening in June 2013. She was named a Columbus Tastemaker in 2015 and listed as #4 Chef (overall, not just food truck chef) in town by *Columbus Monthly* magazine. She has appeared on national television and has been featured in nearly every local magazine consistently for the last three years.

While her professional success has made it challenging to find time to spend with the support system she came back to Columbus for, she says the "rewards are endless" and is driven by the desire to succeed for those that have supported her all along.

LECHON ASADO:
SLOW ROASTED PORK WITH MOJO SAUCE & CILANTRO
Courtesy of Onel & Pam Perez, The Guava Tree Truck

Classically served atop basmati rice, this is the garlicky and grand centerpiece of many Cuban celebrations. The pork needs at least 8 hours to cook, but the results—unbelievably tender meat and crisp, crackly skin—will have you wishing this dish was always part of your traditions.

Serves 4

INGREDIENTS:
PORK:
1 pork butt (trim off some of the fat from underneath), approximately 4 to 5 pounds
1/2 cup sour orange juice (I get this from a tree in my mom's yard, but you can use 1 small can of regular orange juice and 1 lemon if sour oranges are not available to make approximately 1/2 cup)
2 tablespoons garlic, minced
1 teaspoon dried oregano
1/2 teaspoon cumin
1/4 cup salt

MOJO SAUCE:
1/4 cup lemon juice
1 tablespoon garlic, minced
1/2 teaspoon salt
1/4 teaspoon ground pepper
1/4 cup water
2 cups olive oil
Cilantro, for serving

PREHEAT oven to 350º F.

Place the pork butt skin side up in a roasting pan and add marinade over the pork butt and then heavily salt the pork and rub it in.

Place the pork in the oven and reduce oven to 285º F for 8 hours or until the internal temperature reaches 190º F. The pork will fall off of the bone.

Add the sauce ingredients to a blender, blend on low, and slowly incorporate the olive oil until it is all blended together and begins to emulsify. Add salt to taste, if needed.

Before serving the pork, sear the pork on a griddle or cast iron griddle to brown the edges. Serve pork with the sauce and fresh cilantro.

THE GUAVA TREE TRUCK *Onel & Pam Perez*

Raising their son in Texas didn't stop Onel Perez's Cuban-born parents from sharing the foods of their homeland. His mom cooked mainly traditional Cuban dishes for each meal and his dad enlisted Perez's help roasting pigs in the backyard. This exposure to a variety of family recipes and traditions came in handy years later when he met his now wife Pam in 2003. The couple married in 2009 and started The Guava Tree Truck in August of 2012.

Since then, they've been featured on season six of *The Great Food Truck Race* on Food Network, have ranked in the Top 10 Best Trucks of Dallas for the past several years, and recently won "The Chompionship" at The Hub Street Food Truck Derby in January 2017.

It's classics like the Lechon Asado, which Perez remembers eating as a kid and what he calls "down home Cuban comfort food," a fast local favorite. Other best sellers include the Cuban Sandwich, Loaded Yucca Fries, and Cuban Donuts.

With a background in graphic design and advertising, Perez tapped into his skills to design the wraps for both of his trucks and still does all of the artwork and marketing himself. While that wasn't as much of a challenge for him as it is for some, he says weather, staffing, and long hours make for difficulties in pursuing the food truck life. But the combination of creating your own flexible schedule, developing camaraderie with other food truckers, and seeing people's faces when they take a bite of his food keeps him going, even in the Texas heat.

MELBOURNE POWER GRAINS BOWL
Courtesy of Andy O'Brien, Kinetic

No jet lag after this trip to Melbourne. Served hot or cold, this refreshing bowl is a total game changer.

Serves 2

INGREDIENTS:
BASE:
1 cup cooked quinoa, chilled
1 cup cooked farro, chilled
1/4 cup chick peas, chilled (optional)
1/4 cucumber, diced
1/2 tomato, diced
1 tablespoon olive oil
1/2 lemon, squeezed
Salt to taste
Pepper to taste

DRESSING:
7 ounces Greek yogurt
5 mint leaves
1/4 cucumber, diced
1/2 lemon
Salt to taste
Pepper to taste

PESTO GRILLED CHICKEN (IF DESIRED):
2 boneless, skinless chicken breasts
2 tablespoons pesto (store bought or your favorite recipe)

MIX base ingredients together and set aside.

To make the dressing, combine ingredients in a blender or food processor. Purée until smooth. If the dressing is too thick, add cucumber and lemon juice to thin it out.

Rub the pesto on chicken and let it marinade. To cook, sear the chicken on your stovetop using a saucepan or skillet on medium-high heat for about 5 to 7 minutes. Preheat the oven to 375º F. Bake the chicken until the internal temperature reaches 165º F (about 5 to 7 minutes).

While your oven is still hot, roast some asparagus and red pepper (page 173)—it's super easy!

To assemble the Melbourne, start with the base mix and build upwards, adding the roasted red peppers, asparagus, and chicken (whole or sliced). Drizzle the herb yogurt dressing on top or around the sides. Enjoy, mate!

SHRIMP & GRITS
Courtesy of Travis Hyde, Sweet T's Southern Style Food Truck

Travis Hyde would "put this one up against anyone's in the city," and yet is happy to share his secrets embracing the idea of people making his dishes to enjoy at home and thinking fondly of him.

Serves 4

INGREDIENTS:
FOR THE SHRIMP:
1 to 2 pounds Gulf shrimp (16 to 20 shrimp)
2 teaspoons cayenne pepper
2 teaspoons granulated garlic
1 teaspoon granulated onion
2 teaspoons dried basil
2 teaspoons dried oregano
1 tablespoon salt
1 tablespoon pepper
2 tablespoons blended oil
1 tablespoon lemon juice

FOR THE GRAVY:
8 ounces smoked bacon lardons
1 large Vidalia onion, diced
2 green bell peppers, diced
1 tablespoon garlic, minced
4 links Andouille sausage, sliced into coins
2 tablespoons butter
2 tablespoons flour
1 1/2 cups chicken stock
1 tablespoon Worcestershire sauce
1 tablespoon dried basil
2 teaspoons dried oregano
Salt to taste
Pepper to taste

FOR THE GRITS:
3 cups ground raw white hominy grits
2 cups milk, preferably whole milk
3 cups water
1/4 cup butter, cubed into tablespoon portions
8 ounces cheddar cheese, shredded
Salt to taste
Pepper to taste
Scallions for garnish

MIX shrimp and next 9 ingredients in a bowl and allow to marinate for at least 30 minutes.

Heat a large sauté pan to medium heat and render your bacon halfway before adding vegetables and garlic.

Allow this mixture to sweat for 5 minutes before adding the sausage and butter. Sauté for 3 minutes then mix in the flour with a wooden spoon and coat all the ingredients, allowing the flour to toast slightly. Add stock and drop the temperature to medium low.

Cook the gravy slowly for 10 minutes and then add the Worcestershire sauce, basil and oregano. Check how the seasoning tastes, add salt and pepper, if necessary.

Meanwhile, simmer milk, water, and 1 tablespoon of butter; whisk in the grits.

Continue to cook the grits on low heat for 25 minutes, adding water if it thickens too much.

When the grits are cooked through and creamy, add cheese and the remaining butter and mix to together; then check the taste of the seasoning.

Pan sear the shrimp over medium-high heat in an oiled sauté pan.

Plate the grits, then gravy, top with the shrimp, and sprinkle with the chopped scallions.

Note: Blended oil is a blend of 75% extra virgin olive oil and 25% vegetable oil.

SWEET / SOUR / SPICY CHICKEN WINGS
Courtesy of Don Salamone, Burger Stevens

This is inspired by the chicken wings of Rochester, New York. Slightly different from our neighbors in Buffalo, these are sweet and tangy.

Serves 2 to 4

INGREDIENTS:
3 teaspoons baking powder
3 teaspoons kosher salt
3 tablespoons cornstarch
16 chicken wings (drumettes and wings—don't skimp, buy quality chicken)
Sticky honey sauce (as needed, see recipe below)

STICKY HONEY SAUCE:
2 1/2 cups Demerara sugar
1 1/2 cups French's mustard
1 1/2 cups Heinz natural ketchup
3/4 cup apple cider vinegar
3/4 cup Red Boat fish sauce
1/2 cup buckwheat honey
1/4 cup Frank's Red Hot cayenne pepper sauce
1 tablespoon crushed red pepper

PREHEAT a deep fat fryer to 375º F.

Mix baking powder, salt, and cornstarch together.

Combine mixture with the chicken wings and let stand for 30 minutes.

Place 1 cup cold water and a trivet into a pressure cooker. Place the chicken wings on top of the trivet. Close the lid and pressure cook the wings at high pressure for 10 minutes. Remove from the heat and let the pressure drop naturally (this takes between 10 and 20 minutes).

While the chicken cooks, make the sauce by combining all the ingredients in a medium saucepan and simmering until thickened, approximately 10 minutes.

Remove the chicken wings from the pressure cooker and pat them dry with paper towels.

Fry the chicken wings at 375º F for 3 minutes.

Toss with the Sticky Honey Sauce.

Chef's Notes:
Demerara sugar is a type of cane sugar with a fairly large grain, pale amber color and a pleasant toffee flavor.

Buckwheat honey is a robust, dark honey gathered from the nectar of the delicate, white flowers of the buckwheat grain. It has been noted for its health benefits including its high levels of antioxidants.

Both are available on Amazon.com if not at your local grocer or specialty foods store.

BURGER STEVENS *Don Salamone*

After a formal culinary upbringing working for classic chefs such as Joel Robuchon, Guy Savoy, and Gordon Ramsay, Don Salamone became the personal chef for a British pop star and his family in Beverly Hills. But it was a move to Portland in April 2016 that prompted him to take his talents to the streets joining the mobile food community by opening Burger Stevens in June of that same year.

He became a quick local favorite due to his best-selling classic, the Cheeseburger. With custom ground beef that gives richness (from having brisket and beef belly in the mix) to the combination of vegetables (lettuce, tomato, onion, pickles) and Fancy Sauce, Salamone says "it becomes this homogeneous creation," and further, "the fresh crunch of the lettuce, the acidity of pickles, the umami of the tomatoes, the sharpness of the thin, raw onions, and the complexity of our paprika-rich sauce work so beautifully together." It's his favorite menu item too, and he's worked hard to ensure its flavors are "perfectly balanced."

Sharing the same challenges as his fellow food cart chefs—plumbing and electricity — Salamone stays motivated to overcome the issues through cleanliness, consistency, properly executed food, and ultimately, happy customers.

Along with his Sweet/Sour/Spicy Chicken Wings, Salamone also shares recipes for two addictive snacks, a new twist on broccoli (page 138) and a classic corn fritter (page 146).

VALENTINA CEVICHE
Courtesy of Carlos Acosta, Rosarito

While ceviche normally features completely raw fish, this take features a pickling technique, also used for Rosarito's tostada (page 58).

Serves 1 to 2

INGREDIENTS:
4 1/2 ounces pickled shrimp (approximately 1/4 pound)
1 tablespoon Valentina hot sauce (or other hot sauce)
1 tablespoon diced cucumber
1/4 teaspoon serrano chile
1 teaspoon onion

TO ASSEMBLE ceviche, combine the pickled shrimp, hot sauce, cucumber, serrano, and onion. Serve with tortilla chips or on a tostada if desired.

SIDES

BACON WRAPPED MEATBALLS (A.K.A. MOINK BALLS) SLAB BBQ

BACON WRAPPED STUFFED JALAPEÑOS (A.K.A. ABTS) SLAB BBQ

BBQ BROCCOLI BURGER STEVENS

BLACK BEAN HUMMUS EXPLORER'S CLUB

BOEREWORS BITES FETTY'S STREET FOOD

CORN FRITTERS BURGER STEVENS

CRAB CROQUETTES DOCK & ROLL

CUBAN STYLE BLACK BEANS THE GUAVA TREE TRUCK

ELOTE SALAD POR'KETTA FOOD TRUCK

FRIED GREEN TOMATOES SWEET T'S SOUTHERN STYLE FOOD TRUCK

GRILLED ASPARAGUS WITH STRAWBERRY KALONJI DRESSING & CUMIN FRIED HAZELNUTS DESIPDX

HOMINY FRIES SWEET T'S SOUTHERN STYLE FOOD TRUCK

INDIAN STYLE RADISH QUICK PICKLES DESIPDX

KIMCHI FRIES CHI'LANTRO

LATKES CHALLAH!

MANGO SALSA TORTILLA STREET FOOD

MARINATED BEETS WITH BLACK WALNUTS VIKING SOUL FOOD

POTATO SALAD CHALLAH!

ROASTED RED PEPPER AND ASPARAGUS KINETIC

SWEET CORN SOUFFLE FETTY'S STREET FOOD

TROLL SNACK! VIKING SOUL FOOD

BACON WRAPPED MEATBALLS (A.K.A. MOINK BALLS)

Courtesy of Mark Avalos, SLAB BBQ

Moink Balls are taking the best of both worlds and colliding them...Mooo and oink. The smoker works its magic to amplify even a store-bought meatball. You can, of course, make your own meatballs using a favorite recipe and follow the same procedure once cooked.

Serves 4

INGREDIENTS:
12 meatballs (store-bought or premade)
Grilling spice rub of choice
12 slices bacon
BBQ sauce, for dipping

TAKE meatball and cover in seasoning or spice rub.

Take a strip of bacon and split it in half. Take each half and wrap around the meatball using a toothpick.

Smoke at 325º F for 30 to 40 minutes or until bacon is done.

Dip smoked meatball into your favorite barbecue sauce.

SLAB BBQ *Mark Avalos*

Since 2006, Mark Avalos has been building a barbecue empire. Starting as a trailer on the University of Texas campus, he focused on that format until about 2009. Now Avalos operates two trucks and two brick-and-mortar restaurants, the latest of which opened in 2017.

Serving originally North Austin, Avalos was excited to bring his barbecue to South Austin in a brick-and-mortar restaurant as well as for the opportunity to offer an expanded menu including his personal favorite, ribs, which were logistically challenging when cooking from a truck. And it works in reverse, such as with his barbecue nachos, which started in the restaurant and at events but are now also available on the truck. Whether customers are picking from the eight sandwiches offered by the truck or the fifteen available at the restaurant, the best seller is the Notorious P.I.G., featuring SLAB's signature pulled pork and coleslaw.

Avalos says it has taken "a lot of blood, sweat, and tears to get to this point," and time spent "praying and hoping that this was the right direction." He says he recognizes that it's truly about serving people as "they're the ones that will make or break you." He acknowledges that "you've gotta love this industry and love people." He also loves the Austin vibe, the fact that the community has embraced food trucks, and that the city has developed a good structure for placement of the trucks.

And Austin loves Avalos right back with one thousand Austinites lining up for the opening of the first SLAB restaurant. Leveraging the truck as a "driving billboard," Avalos promotes the restaurant both on the streets as well as at events. While it was once unheard of to have a food truck at events like corporate functions, weddings and wedding rehearsals, now it's fun to have a cool street food feel causing this market to be the biggest area for growth and continued expansion of the SLAB brand.

BACON WRAPPED STUFFED JALAPEÑOS (A.K.A. ABTS)
Courtesy of Mark Avalos, SLAB BBQ

ABTs are appealing appetizers with an unappealing nickname...Atomic Buffalo Turds. Not sure where that name came from but that's how they are known in the BBQ community. Once again, smoking adds another dimension to this classic bar snack. Betchya can't eat just one!

Serves 4

INGREDIENTS:
12 jalapeño peppers
4 to 6 ounces cream cheese, depending on size of peppers
4 to 6 ounces pepper jelly, depending on size of peppers
12 slices bacon

SPLIT jalapeños in half. Scrape the inside of each half with a spoon to remove the seeds.

Stuff one half of the pepper with cream cheese and the other half with your favorite kind of pepper jelly.

Merge the two halves together and then wrap in bacon using a toothpick.

Smoke at 325º F for 30 to 40 minutes or until bacon is done.

BBQ BROCCOLI *Courtesy of Don Salamone, Burger Stevens*

This is an addictive snack to make anytime. It's easy and amazing. You just need a hot oven with a convection fan.

Serves 4

INGREDIENTS:
2 bunches broccoli
3/4 cup grapeseed oil
1 cup BBQ rub (recipe follows)

BBQ RUB (this makes much more than you need, but it definitely comes in handy):
1/2 cup paprika
1/2 cup salt
1/2 cup brown sugar
1/2 cup granulated garlic
1/4 cup chili powder
6 tablespoons granulated onion
1 tablespoon black pepper, ground
1 tablespoon dried oregano
1 tablespoon mustard powder
1 teaspoon cumin
1 teaspoon cayenne pepper

PREHEAT oven to 400ºF with the convection fan on.

Separate the broccoli into 1-inch florets.

Toss the broccoli with the grapeseed oil, generously.

Place the broccoli on a sheet pan making sure the florets are spaced out.

Roast the broccoli for 20 to 25 minutes. After 10 minutes, flip the florets on the pan. Continue to cook. The broccoli may take on a char, which is desirable.

Meanwhile, make the BBQ rub.

Take the broccoli out of the oven and using a metal spatula, scrape the florets from the pan.

Put the broccoli in a large bowl and quickly toss with the BBQ Rub. I say quickly because you don't want the broccoli to steam and wilt. Crunchy and charred is what you want.

Devour.

Chef's Note: Convection fan on means that If there is a fan in your oven, it is turned on. This circulates hot air, resulting in even cooking.

BLACK BEAN HUMMUS
Courtesy of Tracy Studer, Explorer's Club

Sesame oil and soy sauce lend unique depth to this cross between a black bean dip and hummus; for a hit of color, garnish with chopped chives.

Serves 6

INGREDIENTS:
2 cans (15.5 ounces each) black beans, drained and rinsed
1 ounce lemon juice
3/4 cup red onion
2 cloves garlic
1/4 cup sesame oil
2 ounces soy sauce
1 1/2 tablespoons cumin
Salt and pepper
Chives, chopped (as garnish, if desired)

POUR all ingredients into a container and mix with a handheld blender. Add salt and pepper to taste.

Serve with pita and tortilla chips.

EXPLORER'S CLUB
Tracy Studer & Orlando Martinez

After 18 years together, Tracy Studer and Orlando Martinez are more like an old married couple than business partners, but the pair wouldn't have it any other way. They've been through a lot owning and operating a Columbus favorite, Explorer's Club, which started as a restaurant in 2011 and expanded to a truck originally for catering. The restaurant has since shut down, and the Explorer's Club has taken up permanent residence at local brewery Zauber but is preparing to go back on the road primarily (as Zauber welcomes new ownership).

Studer loves being on the truck for the flexibility it provides and the day to day change in either venue, customers, or both. They've been working out of the ECDI Food Fort since leaving their commissary kitchen and have enjoyed the camaraderie as well as support in booking catering jobs and festivals.

Over five years in operation, Explorer's Club has built one of the biggest truck menus in the city. Studer says it can be a double-edged sword and is sometimes "brutal to execute." But area vegetarians and vegans love having options beyond the standard salad, and Martinez's creative menu items like tacos, quesadillas, and hummus quinoa patties served with a cranberry chutney are consistent customer favorites. They've also partnered with fellow food trucker Stephen Redzinak of Sophie's to serve his pierogi and Monica Sherchan who handcrafts a potsticker-type South Asian dumpling called a Momo, which encloses a mixture of tofu, shredded carrots, and ginger served alongside a dipping sauce and Asian slaw.

But it's probably the longtime favorite Mofongo sandwich that has fans clamoring for an Explorer's Club 2.0, even offering to start a GoFundMe campaign to raise funds for a new brick and mortar. It's Studer's favorite, too featuring pork butt that's been oven roasted for 12 hours, shredded, and combined with sweet plantains, roasted garlic, roasted whole cloves, cilantro, and lime juice. He estimates they sold over ten thousand sandwiches in one year. He also loves their Cuban, featuring slow roasted pork, sliced ham, pickles, mustard, and sliced cheese. (You can ask him to leave off the pickles, but change anything else and he says "It's just not a Cuban anymore.")

Next up for menu expansion is the roll out of Explorer Bowls that addresses the customer desire for a dish that is a full meal but healthier than a sandwich. Built on a base of jasmine rice, grilled vegetables, and black beans, one can choose to top their bowl with either chicken or mofongo. Studer's even experimenting with an edible tortilla bowl which eventually, he hopes to serve the dish in.

He says the Columbus food truck scene is "getting even more crazy." More trucks are appearing—more than are dropping out, which also brings the addition of "new cuisines, such as South African." With a loyal fan base and an ever-evolving menu catering to a diverse array of customer preferences, Studer sees more requests for weddings, parties, and events like bike races every day. He hopes the shift to returning to the road will free up some personal time and even allow for some time off during the offseason. But for now, there are no signs of slowing down for this long-established favorite.

BOEREWORS BITES

Courtesy of Damian Ettish, Fetty's Street Food

Boerewors is a South African farmers sausage enjoyed all over the country with a braai (BBQ). This is my take on making this ubiquitous South African staple into something every American can love.

Makes about 30 bites

INGREDIENTS:

1 pound sirloin, ground
1/2 pound pork belly, ground
1 small onion, finely chopped
5 cloves garlic, finely grated
3 tablespoons coriander seeds
2 tablespoons salt
1 tablespoon ground black pepper
1 tablespoon sugar
2 teaspoons ground allspice
1 teaspoon nutmeg
3/4 teaspoon ground cloves
1/2 teaspoon cumin
1/4 teaspoon cinnamon
1/2 cup mozzarella cheese, grated
1/2 cup cold white rice
1/2 cup cilantro, chopped
2 eggs
1 cup all-purpose flour
2 to 3 eggs, beaten
2 cups seasoned breadcrumbs

DIPPING SAUCE:

1/2 cup mayonnaise
1/4 cup ketchup
2 tablespoons sriracha sauce

PREPARE all the ingredients up through the cilantro and mix together with two eggs in a large bowl. Let the mixture stand for an hour to overnight.

In three smaller bowls, add flour into one bowl, beaten eggs into another bowl and finally, breadcrumbs to the third bowl.

Using a tablespoon, scoop the meat mixture into the palm of your hand and make ping pong-sized balls.

Roll each ball in the flour, then beaten egg and finally the bread crumbs. Set aside until all the Boerewors bites are coated this way.

Heat the oil to 325º F and fry the bites in batches of 5 or 6 until golden brown on the outside.

Mix the dipping sauce ingredients together in a bowl and serve.

FETTY'S STREET FOOD *Damian Ettish*

After climbing the corporate ladder of an intense London advertising agency, Damian Ettish told his boss he was resigning to travel to India and learn about Indian street food. To his surprise, his boss was supportive even keeping his job for him for the four months he was gone. Upon his return, Ettish took his new found knowledge and turned it into a side business making lunches for colleagues and working his way up to sixty orders per day. The cooking bug had bitten him hard, and he eventually took off again to Thailand and Vietnam for a combined seven months to continue his education in street food and the traditional meals of each of those cultures.

Taking his newly learned culinary inspirations with him, he returned to his childhood home of Cape Town, South Africa, and decided to open his first food truck in an old VW camper. In just a year's time, he became widely recognized as one of the top food trucks in Cape Town and was featured in several print and online magazines. All the while, he'd been in a long distance relationship, and after two years of traveling between Cape Town and Columbus, Ohio, he and his now wife decided it was time for him to relocate. Knowing the mobile food scene in Columbus was well established, the opportunity to jump in and share the food of his homeland was instantly appealing. In a serendipitous twist, his in-laws had owned a Thai restaurant in Columbus for thirty years and were able to help guide him regarding the local restaurant scene.

Since he introduced Columbus to the traditional South African foods of his childhood, he has noticed that "in the last two years, people's appetite for new and different flavors is increasing," and now, "people aren't asking, 'what is it?' as much as they used to and rather, are asking, 'what's it like?'" This open-mindedness led to a classic dish called Bunny Chow quickly becoming a customer favorite. It's a South African butter chicken curry served in a hollowed out bread bowl with cucumber raita. Another instant hit was Ettish's Thai Fried Rice, an authentic stir-fried jasmine rice with fresh vegetables and Thai spices that he learned in a town called Krabi in South Thailand. He recalls, "I spent about ten hours on a piping hot day watching a woman at her small stall making countless fried rices. Eventually, she showed me her tricks and her faithful recipe. By the end of the day, I was cooking her dish for her customers."

Ettish praises Columbus for affording him the opportunity to "showcase a part of me that wouldn't have been unique in South Africa" saying, "I'm able to make food from home and be adventurous at the same time." He's been pleased to find the local food scene quickly evolving and has plans to take his parents and brother to a few of his new favorite spots when they visit for the first time in 2017. They'll be on a cultural tour of the city checking out Momo Ghar for Nepalese, Jeni's Ice Creams, fellow food truck Ray Ray's Hog Pit for smoked meats, and the newly opened Watershed Kitchen & Bar, a place he says is "modern, yet understated and just cool. You feel like you could be in New York, or London, or LA. I believe it's the first of many more of these kinds of restaurants in Columbus." His pick? The smoked bread pudding featuring caul fat, shiitake mushrooms, charred carrots, and crispy lentils. It's unexpected but perfectly at home in the city's evolving food scene, just like Ettish.

CORN FRITTERS
Courtesy of Don Salamone, Burger Stevens

Another addictive snack. The quality of the corn really makes a difference. In a bind or off-season, frozen corn works, but make sure to thaw it first.

Serves 4

INGREDIENTS:
Oil (as needed to fill a deep fryer)
4 cups cornmeal
1/4 cup all purpose flour
2 teaspoons baking soda
2 teaspoons baking powder
2 tablespoons salt
2 cups buttermilk
2 eggs
1 cup onion, grated
6 egg whites, whipped into stiff peaks
2 cups corn kernels

FILL deep fryer with oil per machine specifications, preheat to 350º F.

In a large bowl, combine the cornmeal, flour, baking soda, baking powder, and salt.

In a separate bowl, combine the buttermilk with the eggs and grated onion.

Beat the egg whites until stiff peaks form. Set aside.

Pour the wet ingredients over the dry ingredients and whisk just to combine.

Fold in the corn.

Fold in whipped egg whites.

Drop tablespoon-sized scoops of batter into the hot oil of the deep fryer, agitating to prevent the fritters from sticking.

Remove the fritters after cooking them approximately 3 minutes.

Season with salt.

Serve as is or with chives sprinkled over them.

CRAB CROQUETTES *Courtesy of Dock and Roll*

This is a really fun and easy recipe to make and can involve the whole family, which makes it that much better! It is a Creole take on a traditional crab cake, made in smaller bite-size portions, and is a very popular special item we run in the spring and summertime. This recipe is not exactly what we make in house because we use a couple of our homemade sauces as substitutes for some ingredients here, but it will still turn out as a tasty appetizer for you and your family to enjoy!

Makes about 16

INGREDIENTS:
1 pound Maine rock crab meat, or any personal favorite substitute
1 red bell pepper, roasted, peeled, seeded, and diced into approximately 1/4-inch pieces
1/2 cup corn kernels off the cob, charred on the grill or in a pan
3 tablespoons lemon juice
2 tablespoons of your favorite hot sauce
1 tablespoon Remoulade a la New Orleans (page 189)
Kosher salt
Black pepper
Granulated onion
Granulated garlic
1 egg
3 cups panko breadcrumbs
1/2 gallon blended oil, or other oil or shortening for frying
1 bunch green onions, finely chopped into 1/4-inch pieces, for garnish

SPECIAL EQUIPMENT:
Deep pot used for frying
Candy thermometer

IN A MIXING bowl, mix the crab, diced red pepper, charred corn kernels, lemon juice, hot sauce, and remoulade together. Season gently with salt, pepper, onion, and garlic. Taste the crab mixture and use your discretion. It should be a little zesty from the hot sauce and remoulade with balance from the lemon juice and seasoning. Adjust the seasoning as desired.

Add the egg and 1/4 cup breadcrumbs. Put on a pair of kitchen or latex gloves (or use your hands) and mix the egg and breadcrumbs into the crab mixture thoroughly. This is going to help the mixture stick together when you fry the croquettes.

Pour the oil into the pot and turn the heat to medium high. You will need to use the candy thermometer. The goal is to get the temperature to 300º F. Check the thermometer from time to time while you are shaping the croquettes, and when it gets to 300º, turn the heat down to just above low. It should stay constant, but make sure to monitor it.

This is when the family gets to have a lot of fun! It's time to start shaping the croquettes. Take the remaining breadcrumbs and place them into a large bowl or on a baking sheet. Season the breadcrumbs lightly with salt, pepper, garlic, and onion. To form one croquette, take approximately one ounce of the mixture and shape it into a ball with both hands and place it in the breadcrumbs. Repeat with the remaining mixture until all of the croquettes are in the breadcrumbs.

Get a plate to reserve the finished croquettes. Then, take one ball and as if you were trying to make a perfect circle with playdoh, using both hands and the breadcrumbs press the croquettes around in your hands a couple of times to form an even more solid ball that is now coated with a lot of breadcrumbs and is more compacted and round. Reserve the finished product on the plate, then repeat the process until all croquettes are breaded.

The oil should now be ready for you to use. Work in 2 or 3 batches with the croquettes and drop 5 or 6 at a time into the oil. While they are frying, line a plate with paper towels to drain any excess oil from the croquettes. When the croquettes are golden brown and floating at the top of the oil, they are done. This should take approximately 2 1/2 to 3 minutes. To remove them, use a slotted spoon and place them on the paper towel-lined plate. Roll them around on the paper towel to remove all the excess oil, then season gently with salt and pepper.

Now you are ready to eat! To plate them, take a few croquettes and circle them around a small bowl of dipping sauce. Then sprinkle some of the chopped scallions around the croquettes and plate, and enjoy!

Chef Notes: Blended oil is a blend of 75% extra virgin olive oil and 25% vegetable oil.

CUBAN STYLE BLACK BEANS
Courtesy of Onel & Pam Perez, The Guava Tree Truck

Traditional Cuban style black beans just like Mom makes. Serve over or next to a bed of white long grain rice. We LOVE Basmati. It has a nice earthiness that works really well with the black beans.

Serves 4 to 6

INGREDIENTS:
1/2 cup olive oil
1 yellow onion, peeled and diced
1 green bell pepper, seeded and diced
1 red bell pepper, seeded and diced
1 yellow bell pepper, seeded and diced
2 tablespoons dried oregano
1 tablespoon ground cumin
3 tablespoons vegetable stock
3 tablespoons garlic, minced
1 cup water
16 ounces dry black beans, rinsed and soaked overnight
1 teaspoon salt
1/4 cup cooking wine
1 cup green Spanish olives

IN A LARGE stock pot, add olive oil, onion and bell peppers, sauté for about 10 to15 minutes, until soft. Add oregano, cumin, vegetable stock, garlic, and water and mix well. Add the black beans and fill the pot with water to cover the beans. Bring to a simmer and cook for 1 1/2 to 2 hours or until black beans are tender. Add salt and cook for 10 more minutes. Turn heat off and add cooking wine. Add the olives to warm them up.

ELOTE SALAD
Courtesy of Tony Layne, Por'Ketta

This is a great salad in summer when fresh corn is at its best but can also be enjoyed any time using a high-quality frozen corn. This salad embodies the vibrant flavors of the Mexican street food favorite elote—smokiness, lime, chili, a small bit of spice, and queso fresco. All ingredients may be adjusted for individual tastes.

Serves 8
INGREDIENTS:
8 ears fresh corn, kernels removed or 1 pound frozen corn niblets, thawed
1 jalapeño pepper, seeded and diced small
1 small red onion, diced small
1/4 cup canola oil
1/2 cup lime juice
1 bunch cilantro, roughly chopped
1/2 teaspoon Ancho chili powder
1 teaspoon smoked paprika
1/4 teaspoon cayenne pepper
1/2 teaspoon kosher salt
1/4 teaspoon ground black pepper
1/3 cup queso fresco cheese, crumbled

HEAT a smoker to 200º F. Place the corn, jalapeño, and onion in a small, shallow foil pan with small holes poked into the foil. This allows smoke to permeate the corn, onion, and pepper. Smoke the vegetables over mesquite wood in the smoker for 30 minutes. Then remove them from the smoker and let cool.

In a large mixing bowl, toss the smoked corn, onion, and jalapeño together with the oil and lime juice.

Add the cilantro, chili powder, paprika, salt, and pepper and toss gently to season evenly.

Add queso fresco crumbles and toss very gently.

Plate and serve immediately.

POR'KETTA FOOD TRUCK
Tony Layne

Tony Layne didn't want to do nachos. Customers had asked for them, his kids (some of which are also his co-workers) even begged. But to Layne, it didn't fit his idea of the rustic American cuisine profile of his Por'Ketta food truck. So what changed his mind? Tasting his pulled pork atop a pile of locally made OH! Chips tortilla chips, crowned with barbecue sauce, cheese, pickled jalapeños, and cilantro crema. And they've been selling like crazy ever since.

Layne jokes that he's "trying to get over his ego." He loves the Mexican culture saying that the food is "vibrant, fiery, and passionate." It also "lends itself well to finger food," which can also mean bar food, a role Por'Ketta has taken on since setting up permanently at the new PINs Mechanical Company, a sprawling bar and entertainment emporium featuring pinball, ping pong, shuffleboard, foosball, and duckpin bowling. Taco Tuesdays have also become a big hit broadening Layne's offering to include Asian favorites like bulgogi and banh mi tacos. The latter features pickled daikon, carrot, cucumber, cilantro, and sambal aioli. It's Layne's way of paying homage to other cuisines but in the Por'Ketta fashion—still smoking and pulling the pork used for his signature sandwich but showcasing it in a new way.

Another new signature dish, the Pork Sundae was a happy accident created one hot summer day during a service out at Buckeye Lake. Craving a new option for a staff meal, Layne layered his potato salad and that same pulled pork in a cup, topping it with arugula and pickled peppers. He loved the taste but wanted texture and something to absorb the juices pooling at the bottom. A nearby corn muffin broken into pieces did the trick, and as soon as people outside the truck saw the dish, they wanted to try one. Layne sold a dozen that first day and has since refined the dish for a place on the permanent menu at PINs saying it's a "mobile food from a mobile vendor."

After 15 months on the road, Layne has enjoyed having a home base and finds it easier to anticipate customer traffic flow. A central location also provides more time to concentrate on the food now that travel time, set up, and tear down are significantly less. He misses doing events especially weddings, which he loves but had to give up for the permanent spot. The future could bring another truck or perhaps a catering arm, which could also offer options for a more plated meal experience. Layne got himself back into a restaurant kitchen recently for a pop up at Three Tigers Brewing to do just that, and his Southern revival menu was a great success. He also recently participated in a local charity event, Souper Heroes Food Truck February, where he shared a Tuscan bean soup that, in true Por'Ketta style, was surprisingly meaty thanks to the addition of a slightly spicy sausage.

Layne enjoys being part of events that celebrate the food truck community, saying it's "unlike the restaurant community in that the competitive spirit is still there, but [the] mobile [community] is far more helping." He has become friends with many of his competitors adding that competition is positive because "without competition you become stagnant."

FRIED GREEN TOMATOES
Courtesy of Travis Hyde, Sweet T's Southern Style Food Truck

A staple of Southern cuisine, this classic side or snack turns the almost inedible into the absolutely delicious.

Serves 4
INGREDIENTS:
2 green tomatoes, sliced into rounds

FOR THE WET MIXTURE:
1 cup milk
1/2 cup mayonnaise
2 eggs
1 tablespoon granulated garlic
1 tablespoon dried parsley
1/2 tablespoon dried basil
1/2 tablespoon black pepper

FOR THE DRY MIXTURE:
2 cups all-purpose flour, divided
1 cup cornmeal
1/2 tablespoon cayenne pepper
1 tablespoon granulated garlic
1 tablespoon granulated onion
1/2 tablespoon dried basil
1/2 tablespoon dried parsley
1/2 tablespoon paprika
1 1/2 tablespoons each, salt & pepper
3 cups oil for frying

WHISK together all of the wet ingredients then set aside. In a separate bowl, mix all of the dry ingredients except for 1 cup of flour. Reserve the remaining cup of flour in a separate bowl.

To prepare the tomatoes for frying, first, dredge the tomato slices first in the reserved unseasoned flour, then, into the wet mixture, and finally, into the dry mixture coating them evenly.

Heat the oil over medium heat or to 325º F and gently place the tomatoes into the oil and fry for 3 minutes before turning over gently and frying for another 2 minutes. Remove the tomatoes from the fry oil with a slotted metal spatula or spoon. Place the tomatoes onto a paper towel-lined plate and allow the excess oil to drain off for 1 minute before gettin' 'em in yer belly.

GRILLED ASPARAGUS WITH STRAWBERRY KALONJI DRESSING & CUMIN FRIED HAZELNUTS

Courtesy of Deepak Saxena, DesiPDX

This is a special that I make with garlic scapes highlighting the bounty of late spring. Asparagus is often easier to find, so I've substituted it here. Kalonji is also called nigella by some vendors, and you can replace it with onion seeds. Ajwain is related to cumin, caraway, etc., and you can replace it with dried thyme. Both are available at Indian grocers or online on Amazon.

Serves 2

INGREDIENTS:
1 bunch asparagus

DRESSING:
1/2 pound strawberries, hulled
3/4 cup lemon juice

1/2 cup neutral flavored oil (canola or sunflower)
1/2 cup water
3 tablespoons kalonji
1/2 tablespoons ajwain
1 teaspoon salt

CUMIN FRIED HAZELNUTS:
1/2 cup hazelnuts, peeled, if possible and coarsely chopped
1/4 cup neutral flavored oil (canola or sunflower)
1/2 tablespoon ground cumin
1 tablespoon salt

BLEND all of the dressing ingredients in a blender until thoroughly blended. This will make about 3 cups of dressing. The dressing can be stored in a jar in the refrigerator for about a week. It might separate a bit, so just give it a good shake.

Heat the oil over medium heat. Add the cumin, stir, and then immediately add the hazelnuts. Stir fry until the hazelnuts are starting to turn brown and become aromatic. Stir in the salt and then transfer the mixture to a bowl.

Grill or pan fry the asparagus to the desired doneness. I like mine close to charred. Place asparagus on a plate, drizzle with dressing, and top with the toasted hazelnuts.

HOMINY FRIES
Courtesy of Travis Hyde, Sweet T's Southern Style Food Truck

Paired with Cajun aioli (page 184), these might just replace your go-to potato version.

Serves 2 to 4

INGREDIENTS:
2 cups milk
2 1/2 cups water
1 tablespoon garlic, minced (1 to 2 cloves)
1 tablespoon granulated onion
1 teaspoon cayenne pepper
2 tablespoons butter
2 bay leaves
3 cups ground hominy grits
3 cups sharp cheddar cheese, shredded
Salt to taste
Pepper to taste

PLACE the milk, water, garlic, onion, cayenne, butter, bay leaves, and salt and pepper in a stock pot and bring the mixture to a simmer and allow bay to bloom in the liquid for 5 minutes before removing the leaves.

Slowly add the grits to the simmering liquid whisking the entire time. Allow this to cook for 20 minutes until it has thickened and then add in the cheese. Whisk the cheese to completely incorporate it into the liquid. Then check the seasoning before pouring onto a greased cookie sheet. Cover the cookie sheet in plastic wrap before placing it in the refrigerator for a minimum of 3 hours.

After the grits have completely cooled, remove them from the pan by inverting the pan onto a cutting board. Cut the grits into fry batons or any shape you desire. Toss in a little extra dry grits and then fry at 350º F until golden brown.

Place on a paper towel-lined plate to drain the excess oil. Add salt and pepper to taste.

INDIAN STYLE RADISH QUICK PICKLES
Courtesy of Deepak Saxena, DesiPDX

These are inspired by Mom's carrot quick pickles—I eat them by the jar whenever I visit her. Amchoor is dried unripe mango and lends tartness to the final product. You can find it at your local Indian grocer or Amazon.com.

Makes 1 to 2 jars

INGREDIENTS:
2 bunches radishes (Easter egg or French breakfast), greens removed
1/2 tablespoon salt
1/2 teaspoon turmeric powder
1/2 teaspoon Kashmiri chili powder (paprika, if not available)
1/2 teaspoon amchoor powder (omit, if not available)
1 teaspoon whole cumin seeds
1/4 cup neutral flavored oil (canola or sunflower)
1/2 cup vinegar

CLEAN the radishes and split them in half lengthwise. Thoroughly mix the radishes with salt, turmeric, chili, and amchoor, if using. Let the seasoned radishes drain in a colander overnight.

Heat the oil in a wide frying pan over medium-high heat. Add the cumin seeds and fry until toasty and fragrant, about 20 seconds. Reduce the heat to medium and add the radishes. Cook for 5 minutes, stirring often.

Add the vinegar and bring the mixture to a boil. Pour radishes and juice into a mason jar, let chill to room temperature and then refrigerate. The radishes can be stored in the refrigerator for about 2 weeks.

KIMCHI FRIES
Courtesy of Jae Kim, Chi'Lantro

Pairing kimchi with French fries is the perfect Korean-American gateway for the unfamiliar to experience and enjoy the flavors of Korean barbecue.

Serves 2 to 4

INGREDIENTS:
BULGOGI:
1 small onion, minced
3 cloves garlic, minced
1 tablespoon fresh ginger, minced
1/2 cup soy sauce
2 tablespoons sugar
1 tablespoon distilled white vinegar
1 teaspoon toasted sesame oil
1 pound boneless rib eye steak, cut into very thin, 3-inch slices
2 tablespoons vegetable oil

TOPPINGS:
1/2 cup sugar
1/4 cup distilled white vinegar
2 tablespoons Korean chile paste (gochujang)
2 tablespoons soy sauce
1 cup kimchi
1/2 cup mayonnaise
3 tablespoons sriracha, plus more for serving
1 pound hot French fries
Shredded cheddar
Chopped white onion
Toasted sesame seeds and cilantro for garnish

FIRST, make the bulgogi. In a resealable plastic bag, combine the onion, garlic, ginger, soy sauce, sugar, vinegar and sesame oil.

Add the rib eye and toss to coat. Seal the bag and refrigerate the meat overnight.

Drain the meat, pick off the solids, and pat dry.

In a large skillet, heat the vegetable oil until smoking. Add the meat and cook over high heat, turning once, until lightly browned, approximately 4 minutes. Transfer the meat to a plate and keep warm. Rinse out the skillet and wipe it dry.

Next, prepare the toppings. In a medium bowl, combine the sugar, vinegar, chile paste and soy sauce. Add the kimchi and toss to coat. Heat the skillet until very hot. Add the kimchi and cook over high heat until the liquid is thickened and glossy and the kimchi is browned in spots, about 5 minutes.

In a small bowl, whisk the mayonnaise together with the 3 tablespoons of sriracha.

To build the dish, scatter the French fries on a platter and top with the bulgogi and kimchi. Drizzle with some of the sriracha mayonnaise and sprinkle with cheddar, onion, sesame seeds, and cilantro. Serve with additional sriracha.

CHI'LANTRO *Jae Kim*

Texas is known for barbecue, and Austin has its fair share of legends in this culinary space, but when Jae Kim decided to open Chi'Lantro in 2010, Austinites were introduced to a whole new approach to their beloved cuisine. Kim strongly feels that "we are here to inspire the way people think about and eat Korean barbecue through service, quality food, and cleanliness of the restaurant," a mission that has served as the base of rapid expansion.

From Kim's first truck in 2010 to the current fleet of four, plus five brick-and-mortar restaurants, Chi'Lantro has not only built a customer following but has also grown to employ over 200 people providing both job opportunities and culinary education.

Set up as a gateway to exploring Korean barbecue, Chi'Lantro's quick service format is approachable and allows for endless customization. Customers choose from a base of rice, noodles, fries, or salad, adding kimchi, vegetables, and homemade sauces. Kim enjoys watching customers create their own combinations and has grown customer choices by offering new sauces and healthier options that attract new customers as well as encourage current fans to frequent the restaurant more often. For those not on a health kick, the fries are an unlikely offering. Originally created on the truck one night when Kim was frustrated that the kimchi (then an unfamiliar ingredient to most) wasn't selling, he decided to caramelize the pickled vegetable dish on the flattop grill. Then he paired it with cheese, cilantro, onions, sriracha, and sesame seeds and served it atop a pile of French fries. It was an instant hit, especially among the 2 a.m. bar crowd and remains a customer favorite at both the trucks and restaurants.

Kim values the open-mindedness of Austinites and how they embrace new and diverse cuisine. As the food movement continues to expand across the country, consumer education has grown, and kimchi has even become a household condiment for certain "foodies." Kim hopes to build the Chi'lantro empire even further. Starting with two more Austin locations in 2017, the goal is up to 50 restaurants, which means locations outside of Austin may appear in the not-so-distant future.

LATKES
Courtesy of Catie Randazzo, Challah!

Serve this simple delight with the traditional accompaniments of apple sauce or sour cream.

Serves 4 to 6

INGREDIENTS:
2 pounds russet potatoes, peeled and coarsely grated
1 1/4 cups matzo meal
1 medium onion, grated
3/4 cup fresh chives, chopped
5 large eggs
1 tablespoon kosher salt
3/4 teaspoon black pepper, freshly ground
Oil (vegetable or canola), for frying

PLACE the grated potatoes in a large bowl or other food safe container, fill it with water, and then strain. Repeat the rinsing process 2 or 3 times until the water runs clear, then drain the potatoes, squeezing out as much water as possible.

Combine the rinsed potatoes, matzo, and onion in a large bowl and mix by hand. Next, add the chives and mix again. Finally add the eggs, salt, and pepper, then massage them into the potato mixture.

Heat 2 to 3 tablespoons of oil in a large cast iron skillet over medium heat. Work in batches, so the latkes are not crowded in the skillet. Take a golf ball-sized portion of the mixture, flatten it between the palms of your hands, then add it to the skillet. Repeat.

Cook the latkes until they are crisp and golden brown but still tender inside. Remove from the latkes from the oil and place on a sheet tray that is lined with paper towels to soak up the extra oil. Keep an eye on your oil level; you may need to add a tablespoon of oil here and there to maintain enough oil in the pan to properly sear the latkes.

MANGO SALSA
Courtesy of Walter Eguez, Tortilla Street Food

This is the most memorable of all of our salsas! The fresh ingredients will give your dish a nice pop of color. When choosing fresh mangos, look for some that give slightly with a gentle squeeze and have a sweet aroma near the stem.

Makes 2 quarts

INGREDIENTS:
3 ripe mangos
1/2 large poblano pepper
1 large tomato
1/2 large red onion
1/2 cup fresh cilantro
2 teaspoons salt
1 lime, juiced

DICE all the fruits and vegetables into 1/4-inch pieces and add to a mixing bowl. Chop the cilantro and add to the mix. Add salt and lime juice and mix thoroughly. Cover and refrigerate for 2 hours or overnight.

This salsa makes an excellent topping for tacos and salads, and it goes great with fresh corn tortilla chips. The full recipe will make enough to fill a medium-sized bowl, perfect to take to a party or potluck. For a smaller amount, feel free to cut the recipe in half to yield 4 cups.

TORTILLA STREET FOOD
Walter Eguez and Gustavo Salazar

Look around the streets of Columbus, Ohio—from a permanent warm weather location at Columbus Commons, to a consistent presence on the campus of Columbus State, to two mobile units that operate nearly every day of the year—and you'll be hard pressed to miss the presence of Tortilla Street Food. Walter Eguez and Gustavo Salazar have partnered for five years now, and the pair continues to grow their brand as well as their loyal following in the capital city.

With grandparents who owned a restaurant in his native Bolivia, Eguez has both cultural and family ties to the food business though he never saw himself in the restaurant industry. After coming to Columbus in 2001, he realized how fulfilling it was and saw that "the opportunities to succeed were boundless." From there, it took only an introduction from a mutual friend for Eguez and Salazar to realize they were both driven, passionate people and the pair quickly decided to join forces to see what they could create.

They started out with a different brand, Los Jalapeños, and learned a lot in their first year of operations eventually trading in their original trailer for a larger truck that "could properly house our dream." That dream includes a build your own style menu, anchored by the crowd favorite burrito offered wrapped in a variety of flavored tortillas. Eguez's personal favorite are the nachos, always a festival attraction as they're "huge and great for sharing." The dish, covered in homemade queso, Eguez promises is "no ordinary cheese" and describes it as the "perfect thin yet creamy consistency...that packs a lot of punch without being too spicy." They also offer a multitude of fresh toppings to choose from so that "you can eat them (nachos) every day with a different combination and never have the same thing twice!"

Eguez says that Columbus is not only "the ultimate melting pot as we have people from every edge of the globe with diverse, unique backgrounds," but also that there is "literally something for everyone here. And if you think there is a gap in the market, start capitalizing on it. Columbus is a fantastic city for entrepreneurs!" Eguez loves that "this city is full of go-getters who have created niche products and services to appeal to the wide array of people who live and travel to Columbus." Foodwise, his brick-and-mortar favorites include The Refectory, Hyde Park and any of Cameron Mitchell's restaurants, but he says he has "honestly been most impressed with what I have seen from the food truck scene. These chefs have a lot of obstacles to deal with daily, yet they turn out food worthy of any of their brick-and-mortar competitors. You can always find me in line for Por'Ketta, Mixing Bowl, and Pitabilities."

Eguez feels accomplished based on Tortilla's strong brand recognition, whether it's the trucks driving down the street or an employee wearing a Tortilla shirt. He says it's the "best feeling in the world to know that what we do makes people happy." He's not stopping yet. He has a few new projects lined up including the addition of the Red Secret Photo Booth, an add-on service for private events, and the upcoming introduction of two mobile dessert concepts, Loco Street Churros and Loco Sweet Eats, later in 2017.

Continuously motivated by the desire to provide for his family while educating his son and daughter about the importance of hard work and determination, Eguez's success inspires him to show them how impactful community involvement can be. He's still very hands on noting that "owning a food truck doesn't mean that I get to sit in an office all day. If I want to truly succeed I need to be in tune with my staff and my customers. That means being a part of the day to day activities. That equates to less time for my private life, but the sacrifices I make now will pay off down the line."

MARINATED BEETS WITH BLACK WALNUTS
Courtesy of Megan Walhood and Jeremy Daniels, Viking Soul Food

It's a simple recipe, but sometimes simple is best. The addition of vanilla is a surprising delight. A little bit of chèvre crumbled over the top is delicious too, just don't go crazy or you'll overwhelm the other flavors. These beets will also go nicely on a bed of sweet, tender summer greens.

Serves 2 to 4

INGREDIENTS:
1 pound red beets (approximately 2 to 3 large or 5 to 6 small)
2 tablespoons salt
1 tablespoon brown sugar
1 tablespoon white sugar
2 cups champagne vinegar
1 bay leaf
1/2 pod vanilla
2 cups beet liquid
High quality extra virgin olive oil, preferably with a grassy, fruity finish.
Black walnuts, if available (regular walnuts will work just fine)

RINSE the beets of any excess dirt. Bring a pot of water up to a simmer and add the beets. Cook until the beets easily pierce with a fork. Strain the beets and reserve the liquid. Allow the beets to cool. Strain the beet liquid through a coffee filter to separate out any fine sediment.

Place 2 cups of the strained beet liquid on the stove with salt, brown sugar, white sugar, champagne vinegar, and bay leaf. Bring the mixture to a boil, dissolving salt and sugars. Remove the bay leaf. Split the vanilla pod open and scrape the seeds into the pot; place the pod in there, as well. Allow the mixture to cool.

With the beets now cool to the touch, peel off their outer skin to reveal a velvety flesh. Cut the beets into 1-inch cubes and toss them into the beet liquid. The beets will be ready to eat a few hours later, but it's best to let them sit for up to one week.

To serve, simply put the beets in a bowl, top with generous amounts of good olive oil, and roughly chopped walnuts.

VIKING SOUL FOOD — Megan Walhood and Jeremy Daniels

It's the little things, especially for Megan Walhood, like when line cook Jeremy Daniels set up her station "just perfectly," which really caught her eye.

Walhood, formerly the sous chef of Nostrana, a well-known Italian standout in Portland, Oregon, had worked mostly in restaurants since graduating college in 1998 except with a brief stint as a groundskeeper and a farmer. Daniels graduated culinary school in 2002 and worked in a few restaurants around town before landing at Nostrana and meeting Walhood. The pair shared family culinary traditions with each other, and Daniels fell in love with the Norwegian potato lefse, a humble flatbread the Walhood family grew up with as a favorite holiday treat.

They saw its larger potential as a great street food and quickly realized they had a unique and versatile concept on their hands noting that Nordic cuisine was grossly underrepresented. In 2010, they purchased a 57-year-old Streamline Duchess aluminum silver trailer, named her Gudrun ("she who knows the secrets of battle") and opened Viking Soul Food specializing in lefse and Scandinavian-inspired dishes.

Traditionally eaten with butter and a generous sprinkling of sugar, the lefse can also be used as a wrap as it is in Viking Soul's best selling dish, the Norwegian meatballs with gjetost gravy and sweet and sour purple cabbage. The meatballs are a shared favorite. For Walhood, they bring back memories of her mother making them around the holidays. She'd dream about them all year until she could eat them again. Daniels now understands, and he will eat one every time he goes to the food cart.

Walhood loves researching dishes and creating specials. She always gets excited when the new ones come out. She says she likes to make sure they taste just the way she wants so she can have several new favorites all year long. Jeremy's marinated beets with vanilla and walnuts, which they share here, is one of her all-time favorites.

In seven years of business, they've overcome challenges like learning when to bring in help to avoid burning themselves out. They say that one of the biggest rewards is that they get to produce food they love and hand it to customers who give them that love right back. They keep themselves motivated because "there's always something you can do to improve your business, whether it's better signage, updating menu formatting, [or] cleaning that one corner that no one cleans. There's always something to improve and that's plenty satisfying."

They're grateful to Portland's "eclectic past and proven tradition of embracing the unusual," which makes it "a great place to try out unique concepts" such as theirs.

POTATO SALAD
Courtesy of Catie Randazzo, Challah!

Use a variety of red, Idaho, purple, and Yukon potatoes to make this dish as visually appealing as it is tasty.

Serves 6 to 8

INGREDIENTS:
3 pounds potatoes
1/2 cup salt
2 large eggs, hard-boiled, roughly chopped
2 tablespoons spicy brown mustard
Juice and zest of one lemon
1 teaspoon white wine vinegar
1 1/4 teaspoons kosher salt
1 teaspoon capers, chopped roughly
4 tablespoons mayonnaise
1 cup red onion, diced into small pieces
1/2 cup fresh dill, chopped roughly
2/3 cup flat leaf parsley, chopped roughly

PLACE the potatoes in a large pot and add enough water to cover them by 2 inches. Use cold water, if you do not the potatoes will not cook evenly. Add the salt and bring the mixture to a boil. Lower the heat and simmer until a knife inserted into one of the potatoes meets no resistance, about 15 to 20 minutes. Drain the potatoes and when they are cool enough to handle, break them into rough chunks by hand and place them into a bowl. Then let the potatoes cool completely.

Add all the remaining ingredients into the bowl with the potatoes. Mix everything together and season the potato salad according to taste.

ROASTED RED PEPPER AND ASPARAGUS
Courtesy of Andy O'Brien, Kinetic

Roasting sounds intimidating, but it can be done in a few easy steps. Learn this skill and watch your everyday recipes reach for the stars.

Serves 2 to 4

INGREDIENTS:
2 to 4 red bell peppers, whole
1 bunch asparagus
4 to 5 tablespoons olive oil
Salt to taste
Pepper to taste

PREHEAT oven to 425º F. Line a baking sheet with aluminum foil and toss red pepper and asparagus in olive oil, salt, and pepper. Bake until the vegetables are tender, about 12 to 18 minutes. Let the cooked vegetables cool and enjoy.

SWEET CORN SOUFFLÉ
Courtesy of Damian Ettish, Fetty's Street Food

I grew up with this recipe. My mom even has a dish that was exclusively used for baking this sweet and crunchy summer soufflé.

Makes 8 to 10 portions

INGREDIENTS:
4 eggs
1 cup granulated sugar
1 can sweet corn
1/2 teaspoon baking powder
3 tablespoons cornstarch
1 1/2 cups milk
1 tablespoon butter

HEAT oven to 350º F.

Beat together the eggs and sugar, then add the sweet corn and mix.

Next add the baking powder and cornstarch, then the milk, mixing just enough to combine all the ingredients.

Pour into a 2-quart oven safe baking dish. Dot the top with small pieces of butter and bake for 1 hour.

Serve warm at a BBQ or with your favorite roast.

TROLL SNACK!

Courtesy of Megan Walhood and Jeremy Daniels, Viking Soul Food
Pickle recipe courtesy of Teressa Snelling, chef de cuisine

This cheese spread is pungent, versatile and addictive; you may find yourself wanting to put it on everything!

We serve it simply, spread on top of knekkebrod, which are Scandinavian rye crackers that you can find at your local grocer. We recommend the Wasa brand multi-grain crackers; they are sturdy and thick enough to stand up to the potent cheese spread. Top with a tangy, sweet pickle and you have yourself the perfect troll snack! Of course, the cheese spread and pickles will go great on sandwiches as well.

Serves 6 to 8

INGREDIENTS:
FOR THE JARLSBERG ("TROLL") SPREAD
(yields about 1 quart):

1/4 cup apple cider vinegar
2 teaspoons white sugar
1/2 pound Jarlsberg (Norwegian Swiss style) cheese, finely shredded
1/2 to 3/4 cup allium butter, depending on taste (recipe below)
1 1/2 cups good quality mayonnaise (homemade is recommended)
1/4 cup Dijon mustard, smooth
2 to 4 cloves garlic, peeled, very finely chopped or pushed through a press
2 teaspoons salt to taste
Optional: 1 teaspoon ground white pepper for extra "umph"

ALLIUM BUTTER (YIELDS ABOUT 1 CUP):

2 yellow onions, peeled and finely diced
8 cloves garlic, peeled and smashed
4 shallots, peeled and finely diced
1/4 pound good quality butter, preferably unsalted
1 tablespoon kosher salt

FOR TERESSA'S BREAD AND BUTTER ZUCCHINI PICKLES (yields about 3 cups to 1 quart):

1 pound zucchini
1 tablespoon, plus 1/4 cup kosher salt
1/2 tablespoon brown mustard seeds
1/2 tablespoon yellow mustard seeds
1 teaspoon coriander seeds
1/4 teaspoon celery seeds
1/4 teaspoon turmeric
1/2 sweet onion
1 1/2 cups white vinegar
1/2 cup water
1/2 cup sugar

STARTING with the recipe for the "troll" spread, dissolve the sugar into the apple cider vinegar. Then, mix all the ingredients together in a bowl using a spatula. It will get more flavorful as it sits, so don't be afraid to make it a day or two ahead. It keeps in the refrigerator for a month, but you probably won't be able to keep it around that long.

Put the onions, garlic, and shallots (collectively referred to as alliums) in a heavy bottom pot with the butter and the kosher salt. Cook the vegetables over medium heat until they start to soften and brown lightly. Turn the heat down to medium low and stir frequently; cook until the alliums are soft and the mixture comes together in a paste.

This butter freezes well and will keep for weeks in the refrigerator. It's a great addition to many sauces or simply melted on a juicy steak.

To make the pickles, slice the zucchini into 1/4-inch thick slices and discard the ends. Set the sliced zucchini into a colander. Then place the colander into an empty bowl that will allow space for drainage between the colander and the bowl. Mix the zucchini slices with 1 tablespoon of salt, and then place them in the refrigerator to drain for 12 hours or overnight. The salt will draw out excess moisture from the zucchini so that your pickling solution doesn't get watered down with the natural juices of the zucchini.

Twelve hours later or simply the next day, toast the mustard seeds, coriander seeds, celery seeds, and turmeric. Place them in a small sauté pan over medium heat moving them around in the pan until the aroma of the warmed spices becomes noticeable. Remove the spices from the pan and set aside.

Thinly slice the sweet onion and set aside.

Take the zucchini slices out of the colander and place them in a medium bowl. Mix the onions in with the zucchini slices. Toss the zucchini and onions with the toasted spices.

In a small pot, bring the vinegar, water, sugar, and remaining 1/4 cup salt to a boil. Pour the hot vinegar liquid over the zucchini, onions, and spices, and let it sit until the liquid cools to room temperature.

Once at room temperature, store the pickles in the refrigerator overnight and enjoy them the next day.

The pickles will keep for several weeks in the refrigerator.

TEXAS FOOD TRUCK CULTURE:
Case Erickson and Tiffany Harelik

As they say, everything's bigger in Texas, and that includes the food truck community. Two of Austin's finest food truck event producers sat down to give us a birds-eye view of why food trucks rule the roost in the capital city and beyond.

CASE ERICKSON, PRODUCER OF TRUCKLANDIA IN AUSTIN, TEXAS

I owned restaurants in the Northern Virginia/DC Metro area until 2010 and relocated to Austin in 2011. As a means to expand my consulting and commercial real estate practice, I began following food trucks in 2012 and launched my first Trucklandia Fest (then known as "Truck by Truckwest") in 2013.

You know I have to ask—what are your favorite meals from food trucks in your city?
If I had to pick my top three, they'd be sliders from Hand Held, the Monte Cristo from Hey You Gonna Eat or What, and the Bahn Mi from Saigon Le Vendeur.

What are some local food trucks that have turned into brick-and-mortar restaurants?
The Peached Tortilla, Gourdough's Doughnuts, Chi'lantro, Spartan Pizza, East Side King, Way South Philly.

How many food trucks are there in your city (an estimate is fine)?
About 350 are currently permitted.

Are the local trucks mobile or stationary?
Both. I'd say 40% mobile trucks, 60% stationary trailers.

Are there food trailer parks in Austin and if so, how many and can you share a little about each of the main pods?
Yes. The Picnic at Barton Springs and The Midway in Westlake are two of the parks that have been around the longest.

What food truck festivals are happening in your city and surrounding area?
Trailer Food Tuesdays in the summer months, Trucklandia Fest in October.

TIFFANY HARELIK, COOKBOOK AUTHOR AND CO-CURATOR OF TRAILER FOOD TUESDAYS

I'm a fourth-generation Austinite, believe it or not. So when I introduced the idea of my cookbooks and the Gypsy Picnic (now Trailer Food Tuesdays) to the Austin community, I was thrilled to receive the acceptance from my hometown. The truth is Austin LOVES food trucks. A true melting pot city, every cuisine, nationality, and age bracket is represented both behind the food truck counter and in the food truck lines.

But the food truck love doesn't stop in Austin. Most major cities have a food truck scene in 2017. We still see a lot of traditional taco trucks at construction sites around the state, sure, but we see a lot of unique menus coming out of food trucks in Dallas, Fort Worth, Houston, San Antonio, San Marcos, and beyond the big cities, too.

We had over twenty thousand people at the first food truck festival I curated; that really speaks to Texans' hearts for food trucks. I once got asked to judge the Texas Food Truck Showdown. Held in Waco, this event drew over ten thousand people and food trucks from every corner of the state. Given that you can drive for twelve hours straight and still be in Texas, that's a lot of food trucks driving through wide-open spaces to get to compete in Waco. I have judged events for my friend Case Erickson of Trucklandia fame. He gives ten thousand dollars to the winning truck each year.

The food truck brotherhood is strong in Texas. I've been at food truck festivals where one guy will run out of limes and the food truck next door gives him a bag to get through the festival. I have seen them help each other with everything from troubleshooting generator problems to fixing sink lines and sharing employees. I have seen them come together in meetings to give each other advice, and I have listened to them speak on behalf of their fellow food truck owners to maintain fair laws in their cities.

Food trucks are being invited to be represented at all of the major food events in Texas (not just the food truck-centric ones): Austin City Limits Music Festival, Fort Worth Food and Wine Festival, and Austin Food and Wine Festival are a few that come to mind.

The food truck community in Texas is alive and well. And in my book, it's here to stay.

SAUCES

CAJUN AIOLI SWEET T'S SOUTHERN STYLE FOOD TRUCK

CREAMY CILANTRO SAUCE TORTILLA STREET FOO

PEAR 'N THE ROSE CITY SYRUP OLE LATTE FOOD CART

POPEYE SAUCE THE EGG CARTON

RASPBERRY HABANERO JAM THE EGG CARTON

REMOULADE A LA NEW ORLEAN DOCK & ROLL

TOMATO JAM BERNIE'S BURGER BUS

CAJUN AIOLI
Courtesy of Travis Hyde, Sweet T's Southern Style Food Truck

Just the right amount of spice makes this a perfect pair for Sweet T's Hominy Fries (page 159).

Makes 1 1/2 cups

INGREDIENTS:
3 egg yolks
1 tablespoon lemon juice
1 tablespoon garlic, minced
1 cup blended oil
2 tablespoons spicy brown mustard
2 tablespoons hot sauce
2 teaspoons capers, rinsed
2 tablespoons flat leaf parsley, chopped
Salt to taste
Pepper to taste

PLACE the yolks, lemon juice, and garlic in a food processor and blend until incorporated.

Slowly drizzle in the oil in a steady stream until it is completely incorporated and emulsified with the egg yolks. It should have a thick mayonnaise-type consistency. Add the remaining ingredients and process until completely incorporated. Adjust salt and pepper to taste.

CREAMY CILANTRO SAUCE
Courtesy of Walter Eguez, Tortilla Street Food

This recipe combines two of our favorite Mexican staples, cilantro, and avocado. This sauce adds a fresh finish to any plate and provides a great balance to spicy dishes.

Makes 20 ounces

INGREDIENTS:
10 tomatillos
1/2 fresh jalapeño
1/2 cup fresh cilantro
1/4 avocado
1/4 cup mayonnaise
1 clove garlic
1 tablespoon salt
1/2 lime, juiced

PREPARE ingredients by removing the skins for the tomatillos, seeds from the jalapeño, and stems from the cilantro. Add all the ingredients into a blender and mix on a medium to high setting until smooth. Refrigerate and store in an airtight container up to 5 days.

Use to top meats, especially grilled chicken, steak, or fish.

PEAR 'N THE ROSE CITY SYRUP
Courtesy of Todd Edwards, Ole Latte Food Cart

Portland is famous for its roses and bounty of fruit, so it was only natural for us to want to honor these qualities in an aromatic syrup for our seasonal lattes.

Makes 1 pint

INGREDIENTS:
2 1/2 cups water
3/4 cup brown sugar
3/4 cup sugar
3 very ripe pears
4 roses

PLACE the water in a small saucepan and bring it to a boil. While the pot is heating up, purée the pears and remove the petals from the roses. Once the water is boiling, add the pear purée and rose petals to the pot and then reduce the heat to a simmer.

Let the mixture simmer for 20 to 30 minutes and then slowly add your sugars into the pot. Stir in the sugar until it is completely dissolved into the purée and petals. Remove the mixture from the heat and let it cool in the refrigerator.

After 1 hour remove the pan from the refrigerator, pour the mixture through a strainer and wring out the remaining pulp to get every tasty drop! Serve in coffees and lattes. Also, great with scones.

POPEYE SAUCE
Courtesy of Sarah and Tim Arkwright, The Egg Carton

We also love this sauce on sandwiches!

Makes about 1 pint

INGREDIENTS:
2 egg yolks
1/2 tablespoon white wine vinegar
1 teaspoon Dijon mustard
A pinch of salt
1 cup olive oil or 1/2 cup olive oil and 1/2 cup canola oil
1/2 cup roasted red peppers, roughly chopped (homemade or store bought)
1 tablespoon sriracha
1/4 teaspoon cayenne pepper

IN A FOOD processor, add the yolks, vinegar, Dijon, and salt. Start the food processor on low speed if possible. Let the processor run for 30 seconds. With the food processor still running, add the oil drop by drop for 15 seconds then begin to add it at a very slow stream.

When all the oil has been added (don't rush it), add the peppers, sriracha, and cayenne pepper. Blend another 30 seconds or until the ingredients are incorporated. Add the extra salt or more cayenne pepper to taste. The aioli will keep for a week in the refrigerator.

RASPBERRY HABANERO JAM
Courtesy of Sarah and Tim Arkwright, The Egg Carton

This jam is a great change from the normal sweet ones to have for breakfast or any time of day. Try it on toast or a bagel with cream cheese or goat cheese.

Makes about 1 pint

INGREDIENTS:
1 1/3 cups raspberries, lightly crushed
3 habaneros (large, if your adventurous), seeded and finely chopped
1 tablespoon water
1 1/2 tablespoons fruit pectin
1 cup sugar

HEAT the raspberries, habaneros, water, and pectin in a high-walled pot until it comes to a boil. Immediately add the sugar and stir over high heat until it returns to a rapid boil. Boil for 1 minute, then remove from the heat and place in a heatproof container. Store in the refrigerator for 24 hours before using.

REMOULADE A LA NEW ORLEANS
Courtesy of Lee Krassner, Dock & Roll

This sauce should taste heavily of the Creole mustard with a touch of spice and acid.

Makes about 1 cup

INGREDIENTS:
3/4 cup Zatarain's Creole mustard
2 teaspoons Worcestershire sauce
1 tablespoon hot sauce
1 tablespoon lemon juice
1 tablespoon mayonnaise
Kosher salt to taste
Black pepper to taste

MIX all the ingredients together in a small bowl except for the salt and pepper. Season gently with the salt and pepper, and taste before adding more. If it does not "pop" on your palate, add a little more salt and pepper. Let the sauce sit in refrigerator for approximately 30 minutes so the ingredients can marry.

TOMATO JAM
Courtesy of Justin Turner, Bernie's Burger Bus

This jam can be kept refrigerated up to a week or frozen for up to six months.

Makes 1 quart

INGREDIENTS:
1 tablespoon olive oil
1 1/2 onion, finely chopped
7 cloves garlic, finely chopped
20 Roma tomatoes, finely chopped
1 tablespoon black pepper
1/8 cup paprika
1/4 cup balsamic vinaigrette
1/4 cup Worcestershire sauce
2 tablespoons molasses
1 tablespoon honey

COAT a pan with oil and sauté onions until clear.

Add the garlic and sauté until caramelized about 8 more minutes.

Add the tomatoes, pepper, paprika, balsamic vinaigrette, Worcestershire, molasses and honey. Simmer for 40 minutes or until jellied.

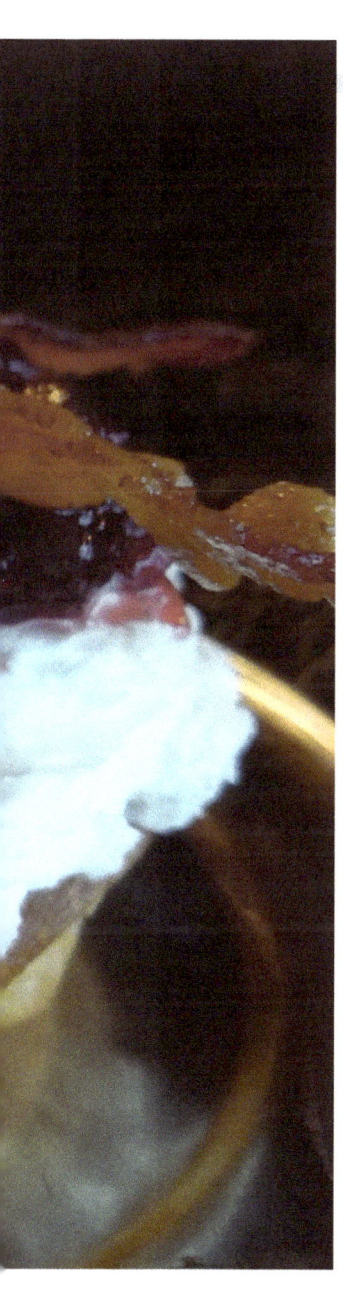

DESSERTS

AVOCADO KEY LIME CHEESECAKE
OMG! CHEESECAKERY

BLUEBERRY LAVENDER SAUCE
OMG! CHEESECAKERY

HAPPY HAVALINA DONUT
GOURDOUGH'S

MS. KAHUHU'S PINEAPPLE CILANTRO POPS
J POPS

AVOCADO KEY LIME CHEESECAKE
Courtesy of Dan Trevino, OMG! Cheesecakery

In South America, avocados are more often eaten as a sweet treat and we decided to try out the surprisingly amazing cheesecake flavor combining avocado and Key limes. Here is what you will need to make a full-sized version.

Makes one cheesecake, 12 slices

INGREDIENTS:

CRUST:
2 cups graham crackers, crushed
6 tablespoons butter (melted)
2 tablespoons white sugar

FILLING:
3 8-ounce packages cream cheese
1 3/4 cups white sugar
1/4 cup sour cream
1/4 cup heavy cream
3 medium avocados, pitted and mashed smooth
1/2 cup Key lime juice

1 tablespoon lemon zest
1 1/2 teaspoons vanilla extract
4 whole eggs
2 egg yolks

FIRST, preheat oven at 350º F. Starting with the crust, lightly butter a 9" springform pan, then cut parchment paper to cover the bottom and sides of the pan. In a large bowl, mix the crushed graham crackers, melted butter, and sugar until it has the consistency of wet sand. It will stick together when pressed between your fingers. Add the crust mixture to the springform pan and form the crust by pressing it into the pan with the bottom of a flat drinking glass. Pre-bake the crust for 12 minutes, then set aside and cool before adding the filling.

Next for the filling, preheat the oven to 500º F. Allow the cream cheese to come to room temperature for a smoother consistency. Add the cream cheese to the mixing bowl and mix on high until smooth (1 to 2 minutes), then scrape down the sides of the bowl.

Set the mixer to low and slowly add in the sugar until blended, then increase to medium speed. Stop the mixer and scrape down the bowl again. Repeat this process with each of the remaining ingredients until a smooth, green batter forms. Pour the batter into the prepared crust.

Once the batter is in the springform pan, place the cheesecake in the oven and bake for 10 minutes at 500º F. Then reduce the temperature to 225º F and bake for 1 hour. After baking for 1 hour, turn off the oven and let it sit for 30 minutes before removing the cheesecake from the springform pan and putting it in the refrigerator to set for at least 6 hours.

Garnish with thinly sliced Key limes and/or our Blueberry Lavender Sauce (page 196) —another great flavor combo!

BLUEBERRY LAVENDER SAUCE
Courtesy of Dan Trevino, OMG! Cheesecakery

One of the most popular toppings OMG! Cheesecakery customers have enjoyed over the years is our Blueberry Lavender Sauce. A little goes a long way and you can use it on cheesecake, ice cream, pancakes, toast...anything you want!

Makes 1 quart

INGREDIENTS:
3 1/2 cups fresh blueberries
1 cup sugar
1/4 teaspoon lemon zest
1 teaspoon lavender extract

ADD 3 cups of the blueberries and all of the sugar to a 2-quart saucepan and begin reducing the blueberries on medium heat. When the blueberries begin to burst, use an immersion blender to blend the blueberries into a smooth consistency, then add the 1/2 cup of remaining berries. Allow the mixture to simmer on low heat for 20 minutes, remove from the heat and then add in the lemon zest and lavender extract. Stir everything together until thoroughly mixed. Refrigerate for 2 hours before use.

Chef's Note:
Lavender extract can be found at specialty stores such as Sur la Table, or online at Amazon.com.

OMG! CHEESECAKERY
Dan Trevino

In one fateful week in 2013, Dan Trevino received two signs of what the future had in store for him. With extra time on his hands after being laid off from a job in the tech industry that had brought him to Austin 20 years prior, Trevino catered a friend's engagement party, bringing cheesecakes he'd been baking with his grandmother since childhood, and took a role as an extra in the food truck focused movie Chef then filming in Austin (you can spot him in line to get food in one of the scenes). During downtime on the set, Trevino began conceiving the idea to marry the two. Not finding a direct competitor in the current market, he decided to turn his hobby into a profession.

From concept to operation in roughly three months, OMG! Cheesecakery shares an opening date with the Thinkery, the Austin Children's Museum, on a particularly frigid (especially for Texas) 18-degree day in December 2013.

Trevino says he has always enjoyed the chemistry part of cheesecakes and seeing the more visceral enjoyment people tended to have for the product. While cheesecake can be intimidating to even experienced bakers, it had always come easy to Trevino. Over the years, he experimented with flavor combinations through requests from family, friends, and coworkers. To further distinguish his concept, he pursued personal-sized portions instead of regular cheesecakes cut into slices and played with shapes and sizes so he could maintain quality while producing large quantities.

Following the successful model of Austin favorite Amy's Ice Creams, Trevino started by perfecting his New York-style cheesecake and offering a wide variety of toppings from fresh fruits to crushed Oreos and favorite combinations like s'mores. He also developed signature sauces such as a balsamic strawberry and a blueberry lavender (which is his personal favorite especially when mixed into the cheesecake batter itself and combined with an extra hit of lavender to take the flavor even further). Other truck best sellers include the Espresso Nutella and Cajeta (a Mexican caramel), followed by seasonal favorites like Avocado Key Lime and specials such as a Maple Bacon developed for the Bacon and Beer Festival and a Mango Togarashi, a spicy concoction created for a wedding.

Trevino credits the tight knit Austin mobile food community saying it's "like a new family," who "looks after each other." He also says that Austinites "really make a point to frequent food trucks and praise" their favorite items, which has encouraged him to recently investigate the potential expansion into grocery stores like Tom's Market.

HAPPY HAVALINA
Courtesy of Paula Walker, Gourdough's

Serves 2

INGREDIENTS:
2 donuts
2 ounces of cream cheese icing (optional for sweeter donut; feel free to use store-bought as well)
4 ounces of no-bake cheesecake filling
4 slices of pan fried bacon
1 1/2 ounces of cranberry habanero jelly
1 tablespoon of candied jalapeños

DONUT (This is not Gourdough's exact donut but a good substitute for home use.) Makes about 2 dozen donuts
1/4 to 1/2 teaspoon active dry yeast
1 1/2 cups warm water (110°F/45°C)
1/2 cup white sugar
1 teaspoon salt
2 eggs
1 cup evaporated milk
7 cups all-purpose flour, divided
1/4 cup shortening
1 quart vegetable oil for frying

CREAM CHEESE ICING:
1/2 cup butter
6 ounces cream cheese
2 cups of confectioners' sugar
2 teaspoons of vanilla

NO-BAKE CHEESECAKE FILLING:
1 8-ounce package cream cheese, room temperature
1/2 can sweetened condensed milk (7 ounces)
1/2 teaspoon vanilla

CRANBERRY HABANERO JELLY makes 3 cups
2 small red or orange sweet bell peppers, stemmed and seeded
3 habaneros, stemmed and seeded
12 ounces of cranberries (about a pint)
2 cups sugar (or about 16 ounces)
1 tablespoon apple cider vinegar

CANDIED JALAPEÑOS:
8 ounces fresh jalapeños
2 cups of sugar
1 cup apple cider vinegar

TO MAKE the donuts, start by dissolving yeast in warm water in a large bowl. Add sugar, salt, eggs and evaporated milk and blend well. Mix in 4 cups of the flour and beat until smooth. Add the shortening and then the remaining 3 cups of flour. Cover and chill for up to 24 hours (3 hours will work if you're in a hurry).

Roll out dough 1-inch thick. Use the top of a drinking glass to cut donut circles and use a butter knife to cut out holes in the middle. Fry in 350°F hot oil for about 5 minutes, turning frequently. If donuts do not pop up, oil is not hot enough. Drain on paper towels.

If you're using cream cheese icing, start by heating the butter in a microwave safe dish on high for 7 seconds. Transfer the butter to a bowl and beat the cream cheese and vanilla extract with an electric mixer until mixture is nearly fluffy, about 5 minutes. Gradually stir the confectioners' sugar into the cream cheese mixture to make a smooth frosting. Store in refrigerator.

For the no-bake cheesecake filling, use an electric mixer set at medium-high speed to beat the cream cheese in a large bowl until smooth. Next, beat in the condensed milk a little at a time, scraping the sides of the bowl, as necessary. Beat in the vanilla. This will go on top of the donut, rather than inside; it's only referred to as "filling" as that is how it is used in a cheesecake.

Next, make the cranberry habanero jelly. Start by preparing the jars for canning. Sterilize six 4-ounce jars in a large pot of boiling water while preparing jam. Place the lids and bands in a separate pan, top with water, and bring just to a simmer before turning off the water.

In a blender or food processor, combine all the peppers (seeds removed) and half of the cranberries and pulse until finely minced. In a wide, heavy-bottomed saucepan, combine remaining cranberries, sugar, vinegar, and pepper mixture. Cook over medium heat. Stir occasionally while the jam cooks down, making sure to scrape the bottom of the pot so nothing burns. Cook for approximately 20 minutes or until a candy thermometer reads 215º F. When the jelly is ready, the mixture should slowly drip from the spoon. Carefully ladle your jam into the clean jars, leaving a half inch of headspace, top with lids and screw bands (not too tight), and process, or let cool. Store the jelly in the refrigerator for immediate use or in the freezer for longer term storage.

For candied jalapeños, cut the stems off the jalapeños and remove the seeds (for milder heat), and slice. Next, add the sugar and vinegar into a heavy saucepan and bring to a rolling boil, constantly stirring until the sugar is dissolved. Once dissolved, reduce the heat and simmer for 5 to 10 minutes or until it is reduced to about half. Continue to simmer until the syrup drips thickly from the spoon or reaches 225º F. Carefully add the jalapeños and simmer for about 5 minutes occasionally stirring to make sure the syrup isn't scorching. If it seems too thick, add a tablespoon or two of water. Remove the pan from the heat and with a slotted spoon add the jalapeños to a clean jar, then carefully ladle in the syrup to cover the jalapeños. Cover and refrigerator for 24 hours before use.

Finally, cook the bacon in a pan until crispy, set aside to cool slightly.

For assembly, top the donut with 1 ounce cream cheese frosting if desired, then 2 ounces no-bake cheesecake filling, 2 slices of bacon, 3/4 ounce jelly and 1/2 tablespoon candied jalapeños.

GOURDOUGH'S
Paula Walker and Ryan Palmer

Gourdough's has become an Austin icon, a beacon of the mobile food revolution, instantly recognizable in equal parts for its adorable Airstream trailers and its awe-inspiring creations: donuts as big as your head piled high with toppings to make them even larger. But whether you're sharing with friends (highly recommended, especially by your physician) or taking on the formidable challenge of devouring one all by yourself, it's the endless combinations that almost guarantee your eyes will be bigger than your stomach.

With the addition of two brick-and-mortar locations known as Gourdough's Public House (both offering an expanded menu of donut sandwiches, burgers, and entrees alongside their lengthy list of signature sweet features, and weekend brunch at the South Lamar spot), the "Home of the Golden Halo" has built upon the "Big. Fat. Donut." success that started in 2009. The growth trajectory shows no signs of slowing down with planned expansion into other markets by the end of 2017. "We are considering trailer locations in San Marcos and Waco and brick-and-mortar locations in the Houston and San Antonio markets," says Paula Walker. To correspond with this expansion, Walker also promises new menu items will be rolling out in the fall of 2017. Keep an eye on their Facebook page for sneak previews. Sounds like a Gourdough's Road Trip is in order!

The Happy Havalina shared here won the Grand Champion prize at the 2017 Waco Food Truck Showdown in April. Doubling up to combine cream cheese icing and no-bake cheesecake filling and then taken over the top by a spicy kick from cranberry habanero jelly and candied jalapeños, it's no surprise this new Gourdough's favorite wowed the over twenty thousand people in attendance and beat out over thirty-nine other trailers in the competition.

MS. KAHUHU'S PINEAPPLE CILANTRO POPS
Courtesy of Steven White, J-Pops

Ms. Kahuhu is one of my best friends and is originally from Hawaii. She suggested this flavor for an ice pop. It is dedicated to her.

Makes approximately 20 pops

INGREDIENTS:
1 large ripe pineapple
1 large lime, juiced
3/4 cup sugar
Pinch of sea salt
2 cups water
Handful of fresh cilantro

CUT and core the pineapple into pieces. Juice the lime.

Place the pineapple pieces, lime juice, sugar, salt, water and cilantro into a blender. Blend until smooth.

Pour liquid into popsicle molds and freeze for 6 hours. Unmold and serve cold.

J-POPS *Steven White*

Steven White may not have known as a child experimenting with the classic Tupperware mold that his fascination with the popsicle would someday become a career, but his mother did. Sometime in junior high or high school he recalls her commenting, "I know you're going to be in the food business someday," as he was always in the kitchen enjoying both cooking and baking.

But Mom would have to wait quite awhile to see her premonition come to fruition, as White first moved to Japan to teach English and then to Atlanta where he first took note of a trend for handcrafted ice pops. He revisited his youth playing around with flavor combinations and bringing them into work until the earthquake and tsunami of 2011 hit Japan. He remembers feeling helpless as he couldn't get back over there to help directly, and so he decided to monetize his product selling pops to his co-workers and donating the profits to the American Red Cross for Japan relief fund.

While others continuously encouraged him to go into business, he never thought it would come to that until he moved home to Columbus in 2012 and realized no one was currently producing anything like his product. Taking a leap of faith, he opened in 2013, capitalizing on the growing local mobile food scene by starting a seasonal cart. He now has a fleet of four carts, two of which are typically dedicated to private parties such as graduations, weddings, festivals, and corporate events. Over the years, he has seen "off season" demand increase for private orders and events, which he is happy to fulfill.

Some of those private orders have inspired special flavors. He's created over 50 flavors, learning what sells and what doesn't and has a core of 5 to 10 signature flavors that he tries to keep on hand based on seasonal ingredients. These customer favorites include Lemon Basil (consistently a top seller), Watermelon Mint, Fresh Strawberry, Raspberry Lime, Passionfruit Blackberry, Berry Lemonade, and Peach.

He also tries to strike a balance for the more adventurous offering combinations like Blackberry Lavender, Honeydew Cracked Black Pepper and Pineapple Cilantro, a pairing that was suggested to him by longtime friend Ms. Kahuhu, who grew up on Maui and helped him experiment to get the right flavor. White's even done Asian-inspired flavors including Ginger Lemonade, Watermelon Lychee, and Cherry Lime Green Tea for the Asian Festival.

White seeks inspiration from all over relying on what's available at the farmers markets and grocery stores and marries those items with his fascination for herbs. While he's not a trained chef joking that he's just a "cook who does what he does," he enjoys working out of the ECDI Food Fort where he is surrounded by true chefs and can use them as a sounding board to bounce ideas off of. One such idea (which started as a Valentine's Day special for an elementary school event) was to dip certain pops in chocolate. The obvious start was with a chocolate-covered strawberry pop, but he's also played around with pineapple banana and will continue to experiment with the offering.

Another new angle White is interested in is local partnerships and collaborations with restaurants and bars to pair the pops with alcohol for a fun twist and differentiated offering. But most importantly, he still focuses on giving back through special days where partial proceeds are donated to charities close to his heart like the OneOrlando Fund, the American Heart Association, and the American Cancer Society and by participating in events like the Columbus Pride Festival.

PORTLAND FOOD CART CULTURE:

Ken Wilson and Steven Shomler

Steven Shomler and Ken Wilson are Portland personalities that are forces of nature. Their dedication to providing good media for the food cart community of Portland is truly special. Wilson and Shomler shared more about what makes Portland food carts a destination the whole world is talking about.

KEN WILSON, MEDIA MAESTRO AND FOOD TRUCK AFICIONADO, PORTLAND, OREGON

I have been in Portland since 1986. I started following the mobile/street food scene in 2011. First, my involvement is as a fan. While my journey started with the food, it quickly expanded to encompass the people who dedicate their time and efforts to running a food cart. It also includes folks such as Tiffany Harelik who are telling the stories of the amazing people who inhabit Portland's food cart/truck universe.

Second, I am a media producer and as such have produced media projects for food truck owners and for authors who write about the food trucks. I also produced videos of on-location interviews with food cart owners. At the time, the idea was to create a web series about food carts in Portland. One of the "webisodes" can be seen here—http://vimeo.com/64197618. I have also created videos for Kickstarter campaigns run by several food cart owners who were raising funds for expansion or brick-and-mortar endeavors.

Third, for two years I was the producer of a weekly radio show called *Tasty Tuesday* at PRP (Portland Radio Project) 99.1 FM that featured interviews with food cart owners. I was privileged to experience a lot of great food and meet many of the outstanding people who operate food carts. Tim Hohl and Terry Travis have been interviewing food cart owners on the *Food Cart Fridays* segment for at least six years (if not longer) as part of their morning show *First Edition* heard on KPAM AM 860. That gives Portland two radio shows/segments specifically about food carts.

Food carts personify on a small scale the values that underpin Portland's culture—the desire to express individuality while remaining a member of the collective and the aspiration to contribute on one's own terms without losing the values and character of the individual. This is best illustrated by those food cart owners who have traveled from as far away as India to open a food cart (Desi PDX) in Portland. They know that their food will be not only embraced but celebrated and made part of the community. They can cook what excites them. They can cook what they choose. Community is the secret ingredient of Portland's food cart culture. Pods become local communities with their own individual culture and aesthetic. It's this experience of community—the local town plaza with food—that defines what food carts give to the greater culture of Portland.

If it's someone's first time visiting Portland, how would you describe the food truck scene and where would you tell them to begin?
I would describe Portland's food cart scene as both vibrant and eclectic. The selection of food styles is nearly bewildering. If you can think of a particular kind of food, you'll most likely be able to find a cart that serves it.

FYI: In Portland, the term is food carts rather than trucks or trailers regardless of the type of vehicle. You could say the term 'food cart' is the talisman of the street food culture in PDX. (There may even be a city ordinance or proclamation or some such about the proper nomenclature for street food establishments—I'm only half kidding here). Get the term wrong, and you'll be instantly branded as an outsider and regarded with the same feelings engendered by invading Mongol hordes or particularly mannerless mountain trolls. Or, God forbid, Californians.

For a first time visitor, I would recommend beginning at one of the larger pods. This will allow the best variety of food styles (within a relatively small venue) from which to choose as well as give first-timers the opportunity to experience the "culture" of the pods.

Do you have some pro tips for people visiting the food carts for the first time?

Patience with the food service at a cart is appreciated and valued. Especially during a rush. The food carts in Portland are not fast-food establishments. The are effectively micro-restaurants. Food is typically cooked to order. So wait times are shorter than at a sit-down restaurant but not the nearly instant service of a fast-food joint.
If you enjoy your meal, be sure to inform the chef (typically the person manning the cart), you'll make their day. They really do appreciate the feedback from customers.

Be prepared to pay cash. While many of the carts do now use Square (or the equivalent), not all have made the leap. Have sufficient cash on hand for a meal and a tip. To be safe, budget your cash at $15-per-person per meal. A typical menu item will cost between $7 to $10, but then there's that cart on the other side of the pod selling Marionberry cheesecake...

Be flexible with your planning. It is possible not all food carts at a specific pod will be open on the day you visit. Mondays and Tuesdays are most often the days on which food carts are closed. The best times to visit are Thursday through Sunday. Typical hours are 11 a.m. till 6 p.m. If you have your heart set on visiting a particular cart, check that cart's (or the pod's) Facebook page, website, or Twitter account for hours and days of operation.

One more thing: Most pods do not have on-site parking. The majority of pod locations necessitate parking on the street. In the downtown core, you'll most likely be paying to park—either at the curb or a parking garage. In the northeast and southeast suburbs and neighborhoods, it's very probable you'll be walking a bit to reach the pod as parking can be at a premium due to popularity and the residents parking their cars on the street.

Are there "food cart parks" in your city and if so, how many and can you share a little about each of the main pods?

Yes. There is even a food cart pod inside the airline terminal at Portland International Airport (PDX).

Many of the pods around PDX have names. Cartopia, Cartlandia, Carts On Foster, Happy Valley Station, Tidbit Food Farm and Garden, Piedmont Station, The Fusion, Cartlab, Portland Mercado, Mississippi Marketplace, Kultural Korner, The Bite on Belmont, Rose City Food Park, Hillsdale Cart Pod, The Gantry at Zidell Yards, Q19, Pod 28, and Piknik Park to name a few.

Those pods without a name are known by their street locations, e.g., SW 9th & Alder, SW 5th and Stark, SW 3rd and Washington, SW 2nd and Stark, NE 23rd & Alberta.

The iconic pod in PDX is the open-air pod at SW 9th & Alder. It encompasses an entire city block. Carts are stationed on the outer edges of a city parking lot. Each cart faces the sidewalk which allows for a leisurely stroll in the core of downtown PDX while making your choices. The SW 10th & Alder pod is literally across the street, in effect, creating a super pod.

A favorite "destination" pod is Tidbit Food Farm and Garden at SE 28th & Division. This is probably the first pod in Portland to be conceived and "purpose-built" with the idea that it would be a destination pod. With several of Portland's best food carts and retail carts on the same lot (an Airstream trailer and a double-decker London bus are used to sell personal items and clothing), Tidbit is one of the most popular pods in PDX.

STEVEN SHOMLER, PORTLAND FOOD CART STORIES, PORTLAND, OREGON

I am Steven Shomler, and I have been writing about food carts and cheering on food cart owners and consulting with them since early 2012. Here is my Portland Food Cart story:

I moved to Portland in the fall of 2004, and I did not go to a food cart until my friend Adam Whalen took me to both the Portland Soup

Company Food Cart and the Lardo Food Cart on back-to-back Fridays in the fall of 2010.

I still remember sitting at the Good Food Cart Pod on Belmont at a picnic table next to the Lardo Food Cart, eating one of Chef Rick Gencarelli's amazing pork belly sandwiches and telling Adam that we needed to start a website telling people about the incredible food you can get at Portland food carts.

The next fall I set out to do just that, and on January 1, 2012, I launched the Portland Food Cart Adventures website. Soon after that, I began to consult with food cart owners (www.FoodCartConsulting.com).
Food Carts and Portland
Food carts have become part of the fabric of Portland. When tourists come to Portland, eating at a food cart is on their list of fun things to do while they are here.

We have more than 600 food carts open at any one time scattered throughout the city. Some food carts are in "stand up and eat" pods like the 10th and Alder pod, and some are in neighborhood pods like the Piknik Park Food Cart Pod in Sellwood.

What is a Food Cart Pod?
You ask, "What is a food cart pod?" It is a place where you will find two or more food carts. Some pods have just two carts, and some have 20 or more.

Here in Portland, the vast majority of our food carts are not mobile. They stay in one place year-round. In fact, mobile carts are actually a very small percentage of the carts we have in Portland.

The advantage of our food cart culture is that you always know where to find your favorite food cart.

FOOD CART DREAMS DO COME TRUE!

One of the wonderful things about our food cart culture is that quite a number of food carts have successfully made the leap from food cart to a brick-and-mortar restaurant.

Teote, Burrasca, Gigi's Café, The Big Egg, Güero No. 1 Tortas, Tiffin Asha, Gabagool, PDX Sliders, Wasabi PDX, Moberi, Ole Latte Coffee, and Phat Cart Café are just some of the Portland restaurants that started out as food carts. It is such a joy when this happens. While running a restaurant is tough, running a food cart is that much tougher.

For example, food cart owners are cold in the winter and hot in the summer. They make most of their money May through October, and many of them then make next to nothing during the more rainy months of November through April. Imagine working in a small box 10 hours a day. It can be grueling and exhausting.

FOOD CART SUCCESS

I have recently launched my YouTube Channel simply titled "Steven Shomler." On my YouTube, you will find two different types of videos: **#1 Spark to Bonfire** videos where I teach about achievement and storytelling, branding, marketing, and social media, and **#2 Success tin for Food Carts** videos where I teach food carts some of the basics that I have seen that are needed to survive.

I have seen hundreds of food carts open and fail, and after more than five years as a part of this community, I know what a "dead cart walking" looks like.

I can also see when a food cart is positioned for success. Here are 5 tips you need to have a successful food cart.

#1 TELL YOUR STORY

You have to tell your story. Get a Facebook page for your cart. Put up an Instagram and Twitter for your cart. No, Instagram alone is NOT enough, even if you are under 30.

If you are going to have just one social media account, make it Facebook. Then once the Facebook page is up, create an Instagram and Twitter account as well.

If you don't have time to do social media, don't worry six months from now when you go out of business, you will have plenty of time.

#2 TELL US THAT YOU ARE A FOOD CART

I can't tell you how many times I have run across a business that I suspect to be a Portland food cart on social media and for the life of me I can't tell that they are a food cart because they do use the words "food cart" anywhere.

Put the words "Portland food cart" in the bio section of your social media accounts and regularly tell your fans on social media that you are a food cart and that you are in Portland.

There are people who are fans of food carts here in Portland who will visit you at least once simply because you have let them know that you are a food cart.

#3 START OUT WITH THREE OR FOUR ITEMS ON THE MENU

Usually, food carts that start out with too many items on their menu usually fail. Five items are too many to start out with. When I say three or four items, I am not kidding.

#4 KEEP CONSISTENT HOURS

If you say that you are open until 7 p.m., DON'T close at 6 p.m. A potential fan will come by at 6:30, find that you are closed and likely will never come back. Food carts that don't keep consistent hours fail.

#5 MAKE GREAT FOOD

It's Portland; if you don't make great food, you likely won't make it.

BONUS TIP #6

If you are thinking about opening a food cart, check out my article How To Have a Great Food Cart Grand Opening – www.HowToHaveAGreatFoodCartGrandOpening.com

LIST OF CONTRIBUTING TRUCKS & CARTS

Bernie's Burger Bus (Houston)
Burger Stevens (Portland)
Burro Cheese Kitchen (Austin)
Challah! (Columbus)
Chi'Lantro (Austin)
DesiPDX (Portland)
Dock & Roll (Austin)
Easy Slider (Dallas)
Explorers Club Food Truck (Columbus)
Fetty's Street Food (Columbus)
Fraiche Mobile Kitchen (Austin)
Gourdough's (Austin)
Hapa Ramen PDX (Portland)
J-Pops (Columbus)
Kinetic (Columbus)
Mangiamo Handmade Street Food (Columbus)
Ole Latte Food Cart (Portland)
OMG! Cheesecakery (Austin)
Paddy Wagon (Columbus)
Por'Ketta (Columbus)
Ray Ray's Hog Pit (Columbus)
Rosarito (Austin)
SLAB BBQ (Austin)
Sophie's Gourmet Pierogi (Columbus)
Street Thyme (Columbus)
Sunnyside Tacos (Columbus)
Sweet T's Southern Style Food Truck (Columbus)
The Egg Carton (Portland)
The Guava Tree Truck (Dallas)
The Peached Tortilla (Austin)
Tortilla Street Food (Columbus)
Viking Soul Food (Portland)
Wasabi Sushi PDX (Portland)

INDEX
Condiments
  Cajun Aioli 186
  Creamy Cilantro 187
  Popeye Sauce 189
  Raspberry Habanero Jam 190
  Remoulade a la New Orleans dipping sauce 191
  Tomato Jam 192
Contributors
  Acosta, Carlos 58, 131
  Acosta, Carlos & Davila, Mauricio 59
  Anderson, James 97, 98
  Arkwright, Sarah & Tim 24, 25, 30, 189, 190
  Avalos, Mark 135, 136, 137
  Burrow, Justin 53
  Cockerell, Joe 86, 112
  Di Bari, Joshua 27, 28, 100
  Edwards, Todd 54, 56, 67, 188
  Eguez, Walter 166, 187
  Eguez, Walter & Salazar, Gustavo 167
  Emrich, Alex 42, 43, 48
  Erickson, Case 181
  Ettish, Damian 143, 144, 176
  Harelik, Tiffany 15
  Hyde, Travis 114, 116, 126, 155, 159, 186
  James, Zach 68, 69, 76
  Kevin Brennan 79
  Kim, Jae 162, 164
  Krassner, Lee 106, 108, 191
  Layne, Tony 152, 153
  Littman, Michael 113
  Littman, Michael & Sarah 110
  Littman, Sarah 110
  Naung, Alex 71, 73
  O'Brien, Andy 124, 174
  Perez, Onel & Pam 121, 122, 151
  Perini, Caroline 34, 36, 61, 74
  Randazzo, Catie 118, 119, 165, 173
  Redzinak, Stephen 63, 65, 89
  Salamone, Don 128, 130, 138, 146
  Saxena, Deepak 92, 95, 157, 161
  Schafbuch, Kristen 40
  Shomler, Steven 11, 215
  Silverstein, Eric 103, 104
  Snelling, Teressa 177

Studer, Tracy 140
Studer, Tracy & Martinez, Orlando 141
Trevino, Dan 196, 198, 199
Turner, Justin 44, 50, 192
Walhood, Megan & Daniels, Jeremy 169, 171, 177
Walker, Paula 201
Walker, Paula & Palmer, Ryan 204
White, Steven 205, 206
Wilson, Ken 182, 209

Meat
  Bacon Wrapped Meatballs 135
  Bacon Wrapped Stuffed Jalapenos 137
  Beef Bacon Cheddar Meatballs 86
  Boerewors Bites 143
  Cajun Flame Burger 48
  Cali' Dreamin' Burger 42
  Chorizo 100
  Cider Braised Loin Chops 97
  Guinness Braised Pulled Pork 112
  It's All Gouda 61
  Jumbolaya 114
  Kimchi Fries 162
  Lamb Bacon 118
  Lechon Asado 121
  Old World Kielbasa Sandwich 63
  Sherriff's Roll 76
  The Al Fresco 34
  The Festa Italiana 54

Poultry
  Brie Stuffed Pierogi with Fried Chicken 89
  Cardamom Chai Chicken 92
  Crispy Umami Chicken Wings 103
  Grilled Hibachi Chicken 110
  Jumbolaya 114
  Melbourne Power Grains Bowl 124
  Sweet/Sour/Spicy Chicken Wings 128
  Trafficking Turkey 68

Seafood
  Crab Croquettes 148
  Green Chile Clam Chowder 106
  Green Shrimp Ceviche Tostada 58
  Hawaiian Style Ahi Limu Poke 113
  Shrimp & Grits 126
  Valentina Ceviche 131

Sweets

Avocado Keylime Cheesecake 196
  Blueberry Lavender Sauce 198
  Happy Havalina 201
  Ms. Kahuhu's Pineapple Cilantro Pops 205
  Pear 'n the Rose City Syrup 188
Trucks & Carts
  Bernie's Burger Bus 44, 46, 50, 192
  Burger Stevens 128, 130, 138, 146
  Burro Cheese Kitchen 53
  Challah! 118, 119, 165, 173
  Chi'Lantro 162, 164
  DesiPDX 92, 95, 157, 161
  Dock n Roll 106, 108, 191
  Easy Slider 34, 36, 61, 74
  Explorer's Club 140, 141
  Fetty's Street Food 143, 144, 176
  Fraiche Mobile Kitchen 40
  Gourdough's 201, 204
  Hapa Ramen PDX 110, 113
  J-Pops 205, 206
  Kinetic 124, 174
  Mangiamo Handmade Street Food 86, 112
  Ole Latte Food Cart 67, 188
  OMG! Cheesecakery 196, 198, 199
  Paddy Wagon 68, 69, 76
  Por'Ketta 152, 153
  Ray Ray's Hog Pit 97, 98
  Rosarito 58, 59, 131
  SLAB BBQ 135, 136, 137
  Sophie's Gourmet Pierogi 63, 65, 89
  Street Thyme 42, 43, 48
  Sunnyside Tacos 27, 28, 100
  Sweet T's Southern Style Food Truck 114, 116, 126, 155, 159, 186
  The Egg Carton 24, 25, 30, 189, 190
  The Guava Tree Truck 121, 122, 151
  The Peached Tortilla 103, 104
  Tortilla Street Food 166, 167, 187
  Viking Soul Food 169, 171, 177
  Wasabi Sushi PDX 71, 73

Vegetarian
  BBQ Broccoli 138
  Black Bean Hummus 140
  Corn Fritters 146
  Cuban Style Black Beans 151

Elote Salad 152
Fried Green Tomatoes 155
Grilled Asparagus with Strawberry Kalonji Dressing 157
Hominy Fries 159
Indian Style Radish Quick Pickles 161
Latkes 165
Mango Salsa 166
Marinated Beets with Black Walnuts 169
Melbourne Power Grains Bowl 124
PB & J Banh Mi Sandwich 67
Potato Salad 173
Roasted Red Pepper and Asparagus 174
Sweet Corn Souffle 176
The Seared Ahi Tuna 74
Treasure Island Roll 71
Troll Snack! 177

Photo Credit:
Amy Ann 14, 203
Challah Team 119
Chi'Lantro Team 162
Devin Hutchins 50
inked fingers 84, 101, 105
Guava Tree Food Truck 121
Heather Marlin 132, 182
James Anderson 97
Jason Hernandez 134, 137
Juanita Gonzalez Valencia 221
Kirsten Gilliam 44
Kristen Schafbuch 38, 41
Kristen Yates 14, 18, 27, 28, 100/101, 102
Kinetic Team 20, 23, 124
Kinzington McElvain 192
Levy Moroshan 14, 32, 54, 56/57
Mauricio Davila 131
Terrance Nixon 117
Tiffany Harelik 139, 140, 147, 172, 197
Tom Kirsch 15
Tony Layne 152
Travis Hyde 155
Sai Moe 14
Scott Mitchell 35, 37, 61, 74
Stephen Lo 69
Stephen Redzinak 63, 88
Steven Shomler 92, 94, 157, 160
White Light Exposure 223

ABOUT THE AUTHORS

RENEE CASTEEL COOK
A Chicago native, Renee first discovered Ohio on a college visit, falling in love with the idyllic college town of Athens, as well as her future husband, while at Ohio University. Without much of a hard sell, Renee convinced then boyfriend and a few fellow Bobcat friends to head back to the Windy City after graduation.

Over ten years, Renee built a successful career in advertising, working at such agencies as Leo Burnett, DraftFCB, and Wunderman, among others. Though a businesswoman by trade, Renee's passion for writing, fueled by a love of travel and exploring cultures through food, now comes to the forefront through this exploration of her new hometown, Columbus, and the opportunity to learn the ropes as coauthor of *The Columbus Food Truck Cookbook* with friend, mentor, and cosmically aligned birthday twin, Tiffany Harelik.

Renee also writes for *Columbus Monthly Magazine*, including features and the monthly recipe column.

Follow Renee on Facebook or Twitter (@RCasteelCook), or visit www.reneecasteelcook.com

STEVEN SHOMLER

Steven Shomler is a writer, author, speaker, radio host and consultant. He is the author of *Portland Food Cart Stories: Behind the Scenes with the City's Culinary Entrepreneurs* – April 2014, and *Portland Beer Stories: Behind the Scenes with the City's Craft Brewers* – June 2015. His current literary project is *Spark to Bonfire: How Branding, Marketing, and Social Media Can Ignite Your Idea*. Steven is writing *Oregon Wine Stories: Behind the Scenes with the State's Winemakers*, as well as *Portland Coffee Stories and Donut Tales*. Steven is also working on the *Beer Drinkers Cookbook: Styles, Pairings and Recipes with Brewer Tomas Sluiter*.

Steven is the festival coordinator for the Portland Spring Beer and Wine Fest, the largest spring beer festival in the US. Steven has been part of the Portland Spring Beer and Wine Fest team since 2014. Steven is one of the co-founders of the Portland Summer Food Cart Festival and he was an organizer of that event in 2013 and 2014.

Steven has a minority ownership position in a Portland startup brewery, Culmination Brewing. He created Portland Culinary Radio which produces the Portland Beer Podcast and the Portland Culinary Podcast. He also hosts the Tasty Tuesday radio show on Portland Radio Project 99.1 FM and www.prp.fm where he has a culinary guest join him in studio for a live interview each week.

He previously worked ten plus years in mortgage banking and ten plus years in the non-profit world including serving for a one and half years as the chaplain for the Cityteam Portland rescue mission and homeless shelter, working with the homeless population in downtown Portland. Steven is the principal at Shomler Consulting. You can follow his adventures at www.StevenShomler.com, and he can be found on Facebook, Twitter, and Instagram.

www.TheSpeakerYouWant.com   www.SparkToBonfire.com

www.PortandBeerPodcast.com
www.PortlandCulinaryPodcast.com
www.PortandFoodCartAdventures.com
www.GreatFoodGreatStories.com
www.PortandBeerFestivals.com
www.PortlandBLTWeek.com
www.StevenShomler.com

TIFFANY HARELIK

Tiffany Harelik (rhymes with garlic) is a native Texan author who has over a dozen cookbooks in her boutique collection of culinary-travel books. She has lectured on food culture and publishing all over the globe including engagements in Europe, the Caribbean, and the United States. She has conducted book signings at world-famous bookstores including Powell's, Book People, The Book Loft, and Barnes and Noble. Her portfolio includes *The Trailer Food Diaries* series, *The Big Bend Cookbook, The Terlingua Chili Cookbook* and *The Big Country Cookbook*. She recently launched Spellbound Publishers in 2016 and is currently building Spellbound Radio.

Born in Austin, Texas and raised in Buffalo Gap, Tiffany is a former rattlesnake roundup queen who is Texas to the bone. Before she began a career in publishing, she earned a Master's Degree in Health Psychology and spent nearly twenty years in event production for corporate clients such as Google, ACL Music Fest, Lollapalooza, Torchy's, Viva Big Bend, Green Fern Events, Trailer Food Tuesdays, and more. When she is not thumbing through cookbooks, she is sipping Sherpa chai on her yoga mat or sailing her way through the islands. She advocates for sobriety, dog rescue, and the conservation of wild places. Follow her as she travels through the universe looking for good ghost stories and recipes just itching to be passed down.
www.tiffanyharelik.com @TiffanyHarelik

www.ingramcontent.com/pod-product-compliance
Lightning Source LLC
Chambersburg PA
CBHW040333300426
44113CB00021B/2743